Breathe Well, Be Well

A Program to Relieve Stress, Anxiety, Asthma, Hypertension, Migraine, and Other Disorders for Better Health

ROBERT FRIED, Ph.D.

John Wiley & Sons, Inc.

New York · Chichester · Weinheim · Brisbane · Singapore · Toronto

Library of Congress Cataloging-in-Publication Data

Fried, Robert
    Breathe well, be well : a program to relieve stress, anxiety, asthma,
    hypertension, migraine, and other disorders for better health /
    Robert Fried.
        p.   cm.
    Includes index.
    ISBN   0-471-32436-1 (paper)
    1. Breathing exercises—Therapeutic use.   2. Stress management.
    I. Title.
    RA782.F75   1999
    615.8'36—dc21   99-12271
                                                                         CIP

DEDICATION

This book is dedicated to Charles M. (Chuck) Stroebel, Ph.D., M.D., a well-known and highly respected pioneer in the behavioral medicine approach to treatment of stress and anxiety disorders, and truly a one-of-a-kind friend.

Sadly, on April 10, 1998, Chuck Stroebel passed away in Andover, Connecticut. I wonder what he would have said about this book, but I am sure that he would have liked it. Few outside the fold know that science is really a dog-eat-dog business where other people's research grants and reputations are targets of opportunity. Chuck Stroebel fell outside that fold. He was a dedicated scientist, a dedicated clinician, and a dedicated friend. He is a great loss to behavioral medicine and to me.

You breathe,
Frosting mountains white,
Exciting trees to verdant flame,
Dancing sparrows on your wing,
Swirling waves into long sighs.
You breathe
And all things live.

Breath is a central concept for Tao.

CONTENTS

v

PART TWO: Taking Action to Feel Better

PART FOUR: Music, Breathing, and Relaxation

PREFACE

In 1990, I wrote *The Breath Connection*, mostly for my clients as a portable condensation of what we did together in therapy sessions at the Stress and Biofeedback Clinic of the Albert Ellis Institute for Rational Emotive and Behavior Therapy (IREBT) in New York City. I am still in practice there, and I try to help individuals who suffer from conventional stress, anxiety, and emotional problems, as well as breathing disorders such as asthma and chronic hyperventilation.

The idea was that my clients could refer to the book when they needed to refresh their memory about facts and techniques intended to help them feel better. I had also intended to give them some additional audio materials on cassette so that they could enhance their training sessions with some recorded self-help instructions and suggestions. The book was intended as a supplement to the breathing assessment and training techniques which were often an integral part of our sessions together.

The book actually ended up being considerably more successful than my audio efforts, and I decided to leave the latter to experts. Here's why.

In the summer of 1988, on one of a number of camping trips to explore the remote arctic Ellesmere Island, in the Canadian Northwest Territories, I took along a tape recorder with the intention of recording the purest sounds, made by the purest babbling brook that I could find, so that I could include those in a proposed audiotape combining nature sounds, music, and breathing instructions to help my clients relax.

It was there that in the serenity of a beautiful arctic morning, only a snowball's throw from the North Pole, and surrounded by the "spirit of the wolves," the awesome truth was revealed to me that the sounds made by a babbling brook are indistinguishable from those made by bacon frying in a pan! As the bacon sizzled, the audiotape project fizzled.

In the You can't please everybody department, it is said that Frank Netter, M.D., the famed medical illustrator, once complained that artists dismissed him as an anatomist, while anatomists dismissed him as an artist. Likewise, some critics from pulmonary medicine have, on occasion, taken my books on breathing to task, claiming that my science is just a little too soft to suit them, while therapists-practitioners have criticized me for being too scientific.

Fortunately, a number of excellent recent books on breathing, such as *The Way of Qigong*, by Kenneth S. Cohen, and *The Breathing Book*, by Donna Farhi, have included my work along with theirs in a repudiation of that criticism. The fact that *The Breath Connection* sold out confirms that the techniques I teach are user-friendly and therapeutic. Keep in mind that much of what is valuable in this book also appeared in *The Breath Connection*, but has been revised and updated for today's reader. I have used composites in writing the stories of my patients.

ACKNOWLEDGMENTS

I have a number of persons to thank for making the publication of this book possible. My charming, brilliant, enthusiastic, mostly good-humored, and ever persevering literary agent, Alice F. Martell, is absolutely unique: half the time she tells me how wonderful my work is, then she gets someone else to rewrite it! Wasn't that Joseph Conrad's complaint?

Alice convinced Tom Miller, my editor at John Wiley, to publish this book. At first, I thought that Tom really liked my book until he returned the manuscript for revision having scribbled CUT . . . CUT all over it! It was slash-and-burn, Tom, just like Caesar in Gaul. Little was left standing. The reader will surely benefit from your helpful suggestions because now, for one thing, the book actually weighs less and, for another thing, it may even read better. Thanks.

I'd be in real trouble if I didn't acknowledge my adoring wife, Virginia L. Cutchin, somewhere in here. It is customary, you know. It is conventionally the case that such an acknowledgment concerns the loved one's patience while the author was slaving away at the keyboard—a sort of metaphoric bone routinely thrown to the loyal dog lying faithfully at your feet. Actually, it is quite the opposite here: I whiled away endless hours writing this book while waiting patiently for her to become proficient in spoken and written Mandarin Chinese, of all things. Thank God she's proficient now and I can finally stop writing.

I should also mention that this book results in large part from the many inquiries that I've received from the public all over the country, and even some from abroad. "Hello! Hello! Is this Dr. Fried? Really? Dr. Fried, please, where can I get a copy of your book? I can't find a copy of your book in any bookstore!" came the recent frantic call from the United Kingdom. "Calm yourself, Madam. Take a slow, deep breath. I'm working on it," I replied.

I already thanked all the many other people who made *The Breath Connection* possible in that book, and this is an updated revision of it. So, that's it.

But I do have a special debt of gratitude—one that I can never repay—to my late friend and colleague Charles (Chuck) Stroebel, Ph.D., M.D. Chuck was a pioneer in the behavioral medicine approach to treating stress and anxiety disorders, and he was well known to its practitioners.

He had such admiration for this work on breathing—and faith in it as a therapeutic element—that, in the foreword to another one of my books, he compared me to Albert Einstein—favorably. Some thought he went overboard. Of course, I modestly disagreed.

How many people can claim a fan like that? His memory endures, though he is no longer with us to give us his unqualified support, and his unvarnished enthusiasm. And that's why this book is dedicated to him.

PART ONE

How Your Breathing Works

CHAPTER 1

You Want to Be Well, Don't You?

Get in Tune . . . Get the Rhythm

Breathing for health happens in the here and now. To breathe for health you must be right here, right now. You can't be somewhere else, at some other time. Let me explain.

When you recall the pain of the past, or you contemplate the unknowns of the future, you are in a sense breathing there and then, and "there-then" breathing obliterates its natural rhythm. But everything in the world both has rhythm and also depends on rhythm. Every particle of the universe has rhythmic motion. Your body has countless rhythms, all of which are the collective action of the individual rhythms of its many little parts. The seasons are a rhythm, the ocean tide has a rhythm, your brain has rhythm, your heart beats rhythmically, and so on. All kinds of things in your body pulsate rhythmically.

Your breath gets its rhythm from your body and, in turn, your breath returns its rhythm to your body. When you lose that natural body-breath rhythm you're in trouble. You may lose mental focus, and memory may falter. You may experience fear, anxiety, stress, even depression. And many other conditions, both mental and physical, that plague you may become aggravated as your body diverts energy to cope with the stress caused by that loss of rhythm.

An ancient Tibetan saying has it that "Breath is the horse and mind is the rider." By controlling your breath, you will learn to master your thoughts and, in so doing, you will master your emotions and control your body as well.

We exist in an unshakable yet invisible time continuum, somewhere between the past and the future. Fear is the tug of past unpleasantness, while anxiety is the tug of anticipated future unpleasantness. We cannot ordinarily free ourselves from the tug exerted by both ends—except by using the rhythm of breathing to bring us back to the here and now.

To master breathing, you will need to learn to shake that timeline and, for a time, to reenter the present, temporarily unburdening yourself of the baggage of the past and the uncertainties of the future. In this book, I will show you how to do that.

Spending a little time in the here and now created by your imagination, when you have mastered the techniques described in this book, may help you to relax and achieve calm in the middle of tumult and chaos, thus allowing your mind to refocus on solving the problems at hand, and your body to regroup its energy resources. It may also help you, as it has many of the clients to whom I have taught the techniques, to overcome many psychological and physical problems and to finally feel well.

First, there are a few things about your body that you will need to know, but I will keep these to a minimum. After all, you don't need to know how an internal combustion engine works in order to drive your car. But you do need to know how to start it, how to steer it, how to fuel it, and how to stop it . . . and, don't forget, where to park it!

Jason lives in the suburbs of a large and cosmopolitan northeastern city. At forty-two years of age, he is a successful lawyer—an associate in a large commercial law firm. He married Nancy, the sister of a close friend, a woman whom he'd known for many years, and he is happy in his marriage to her. Jason and Nancy have three school-age children. Both he and Nancy exercise regularly and they watch their diet.

Yet, on the occasion of Jason's last periodic medical checkup, his physician informed him that his blood pressure was borderline elevated at 145/85 mm Hg (millimeters of mercury), and that he was ordering him to have a blood test to assess his cholesterol level. If in the normal range, his blood pressure would not be expected to exceed 115/80. Furthermore, his physician informed him that while his blood pressure was not yet dangerously elevated, he might have to consider medication, depending on the cholesterol results.

Jason asked him what kind of medication might be required and why it was needed, if his blood pressure was only borderline elevated. His doctor replied that it was too early to tell, but that even modestly elevated cholesterol is one of the major causes of high blood pressure and that, at present, there was no other obvious explanation for his elevated blood pressure. His doctor then prescribed the usual nostrum: cautioning him to slow down because blood pressure is also known to rise with stress.

Carol lives in an East Coast city and works in a fashionable boutique located in a large shopping mall. She is thirty-four years old and, because she is recently divorced, she must also shoulder the duties and responsibilities of bringing up two small children and caring for her home. Although she is in generally good health, she has had a prior history of occasional severe headaches, usually aggravated just before her period. But she now experiences these headaches much more frequently, and the analgesics she takes to reduce the pain seem to be becoming gradually less effective. Such headaches have been a hallmark in her family, and she will tell you that her mother reported more than occasional relentless head pain. Nevertheless, she attributes her headaches to stress.

Karl is a seventeen-year-old high school student and a would-be athlete who grew up in a small midwestern city. As a youngster he had several relatively mild, albeit alarming, episodes of asthma. His attacks were not severe, and he was given medication that kept them pretty well in check. Karl considered himself fortunate because, as he grew up and matured, his asthma attacks became increasingly less frequent and, it would seem, they finally disappeared.

Karl's family could not afford to send him to college, but his meteoric high school track career came to the attention of a scout who was able to secure a sports scholarship for him at a well-known university. But Karl experienced episodes of breathlessness which caused him to cancel practice sessions. Karl was referred to a physician who examined him and reported that he had asthma. Karl, like many persons, has a sort of latent asthma that can be triggered by exercise.

Mark is an aspiring concert violinist. Though he is an accomplished musician, his hands freeze before each performance and he fears that he will not be able to perform. He would like to be able to find a way to warm his hands and to reduce the excruciating anxiety he experiences before each performance.

What these persons and the many others who have sought treatment or breathing training with me have in common is that the breathing techniques which I developed helped them to overcome their condition—either by entirely eliminating it or by significantly reducing the symptom frequency and severity.

What's Different About This Breathing Program?

I developed the breathing retraining program described in this book while I was director of the Rehabilitation Research Institute at the International Center for the Disabled in New York City. As its effectiveness became increasingly more obvious, I included it in the treatment of a variety of our outpatients, and I also began to report it at scientific conferences. As scientific and media news about the effectiveness of this breathing retraining method began to spread, I was invited to teach it to health care professionals both in the United States and abroad.

What made this technique effective and unique is that it normalized the oxygen and carbon dioxide gas levels in the blood and in the body, thus restoring the normal balance of the body and the normal rhythm of breath and heart. In a word, it normalized metabolism. How was this done?

Scientific instruments were used during breathing training to measure different physiological functions such as pulse rate, lung and blood oxygen content, muscle tension, and blood flow in the body. During the breathing training sessions, the patients were fitted with special sensors that allowed me to observe their chest and abdomen motion at the same time as I observed the physiological functions mentioned above.

This complex set of simultaneous observations made it possible for me to fine-tune the instructions to patients during the training so that a particular final set of instructions emerged. That set of instructions, contained in this book, transforms a disordered breath-heart pattern with abnormal body and brain oxygen and carbon dioxide levels to a normal rhythm indicative of relaxation and well-being.

The Holistic or Complementary Approach

My clients are not simply examples of disordered metabolism. They have existential problems that either result from that disordered metabolism or cause it. Thus, besides doing breathing and relaxation exercises, my clients and I talk about the best way in which they can help themselves to reduce their suffering by learning everything possible about their condition. Every shred of information is important: it forms part of a total picture of their condition, and it helps them to know what questions to ask me and what answers to expect.

Some also come to me for training for nonclinical reasons, such as improving athletic performance, voice control, and so on. But, for the most part, many of my clients suffer from anxiety, stress, and psychosomatic disorders, and they may also be in therapy with a primary therapist who helps them with their emotional or psychological problems. "Psychosomatic" is an archaic term left over from the psychoanalytic concept of hysteria. It means physical manifestation(s) of emotional conflicts. Typically, these clients are referred to me for help with the somatic aspects of their disorders, such as muscle tension–related pain, anxiety, panic attacks, insomnia, and chronic pain, as well as various preexisting medical disorders that are acknowledged to be aggravated by stress and anxiety: high blood pressure, migraine, headaches, hyperventilation, asthma, ulcers/gastritis, colitis, and allergies, among others.

Treatment often combines breathing retraining (with music and mental imagery) with cognitive coping strategies. Therefore, it is not by coincidence that I now practice at the Albert Ellis Institute for Rational Emotive and Behavior Therapy. The Institute philosophy is that of *rational emotive therapy* (RET), a cognitive behavior therapy consistent with the teachings of its founder, Albert Ellis.

Breathing training often complements RET because it is a form of behavior therapy. It is not cognitive, but it teaches clients to reduce their anxiety, stress, and pain by adopting rational counterstress strategies by behavioral self-regulation. Anxiolytic (antianxiety) drugs can constitute a counterstress strategy. Thus I specify here those that are behavioral.

The theory underlying RET asserts that one may be victimized by irrational thinking, and the theory underlying this form of breath control asserts that one may also be victimized by maladaptive muscle and body patterns due to stress, which can both cause maladaptive patterns and be caused by them. Some of these patterns we call *dysponesis*. An example of this is the partial contraction of the diaphragm observed in persons with chronic pain.

Biofeedback and relaxation therapy follow the principles of behavioral medicine. Daniel Goleman defines behavioral medicine as a medical field whose techniques use the mind of the patient to help heal his/her body.[1] This definition is only partly correct: most of its techniques do not come from medicine, but from psychology. In fact, much to your disadvantage, the techniques of behavioral medicine have until recently been mostly either ignored or criticized by establishment medicine.

Behavioral medicine is a comprehensive approach to treatment, focusing also on the personal, motivational, and social aspects of illness. It poses the questions:

- Are you motivated to be/get well?
- Are you willing to comply with a "behavioral treatment contract"?
- What factors in your social or family context contribute to maintaining your disorder?
- What are the different meanings that your disorder has for you?
- What role might the disorder play in your life?
- What secondary problems are created by your disorder or by your coping strategies?

For instance, you may have a long history of migraine and wish to try biofeedback treatment. Although medication helped at first, it no longer does.

After having the nature of the disorder explained to you, and the multifactor approach to its treatment, you may well show up for every training session but will not adhere to the practice exercises and nutritional or other guidelines essential to a satisfactory outcome, despite the considerable pain and misery of this disorder. Some persons simply may not do what is essential to part with symptoms.

Sometimes a symptom may play a vital role in your life. It may be a family rallying point, a source of sympathy or otherwise scarce attention and affection, or a means of avoiding unpleasant tasks. If that turns out to be the case, it becomes essential for you to learn coping skills and make lifestyle changes so that support for the disorder will be neutralized.

Conventional medicine lacks the inclination to address such issues. The aim of conventional medicine is to *cure* with medication or with surgery. Behavioral medicine, on the other hand, focuses on the interaction between the individual psychology of the person and his/her social milieu and physical conditions.

Breathing retraining is only one of the methods of behavioral medicine. Biofeedback treatment also requires a look at your self-image, your family, your symptoms history, how you cope, how you live, what you like and dislike, what you eat, if you exercise, and many other factors, including your hopes and fears. And from all of this information, a strategy of treatment by self-regulation is fashioned for you.

Self-regulation means that getting well may include methods that you can use yourself—for instance, controlling breathing or relaxing to overcome muscle tension or high blood pressure, controlling hand temperature, or eating habits all can help you to overcome migraine, or the spasms of Raynaud's disease.

There are few conditions treated with conventional medication that cannot also be treated with one or more of the self-regulation/ biofeedback strategies. But medication is often more rapid, and it certainly is more convenient, though it may have hazardous side effects.

This point is underscored by an article in the *New England Journal of Medicine*.[2] Many forms of heart disease and hypertension have been successfully treated with behavioral methods such as biofeedback, relaxation, and yoga, which entail no hazardous side effects.

Many of you who are familiar with relaxation and yoga may not know what biofeedback is. Biofeedback is a set of techniques in which instruments, usually attached to various parts of the body, are used to observe an involuntary body function which one is trying to learn to control. Instruments feed the information back to the learner so that s/he can see the outcome of his or her efforts. For instance, if you wish to learn to relax your shoulder muscles with biofeedback, sensors would be placed over the right and left shoulder muscles about midway between your shoulder and your neck.

In one form of biofeedback, a tone whose pitch rises and falls as tension rises and falls, indicates to you when, by trial and error, you are either raising or lowering the tension in those muscles. We have found over the years that this is an effective way to learn muscle relaxation: trial and error with biofeedback.

But the breathing training described in this book is not based on trial and error, but on guided exercises.

The Breath Connection

Whether we are rehabilitation medicine breathing trainers or psychologists in biofeedback practice, we all recognize a two-way relationship between the physiological condition of the body and the brain—the way that the body organs and brain interact. It is doubtful that anyone would stake his or her reputation on the truth of either of the following statements: "It is the mind that affects the body," or "It is the body that affects the mind."

But today, most therapists are trained to know something about both the workings of the body they are helping to train and the psychology of the person in whom these systems have faltered. They know about the role of learning (conditioning), ideas (cognition), social context, and expectations. And now they are learning about the role of breathing—certain types of breathing can make you ill, others can make you well.

Frequently, when you are disturbed, you may note certain characteristic breathing changes. And conversely, when your mental state or mood changes, your breathing may change along with it. This has been known for thousands of years and is being rediscovered every day in medical and psychology laboratories all over the world. These breathing changes may become chronic, and they may create new physical or emotional disorders of their own accord.

Perhaps you, or someone you know well, has been said to be stressed-out, or even neurotic. But what does "stressed-out" or "neurotic" really mean? Were you said to be anxious? Do you have phobias? Panic attacks? Do you have strange, unexplainable symptoms such as dizziness and/or weakness, which your physician dismisses as "all in your head"?

I'll bet whatever your complaints, they are accompanied by some kind of abnormal breathing pattern: perhaps rapid, shallow breaths, heaving sighs, or breathlessness. If that's all it is, you may take comfort from the fact that medicine has shown that people with these symptoms will likely outlive their doctor's office staff.

These symptoms that medicine says are all in your head traditionally make up the so-called *psychosomatic disorders*. Well, I have spent the past fifteen years studying the role of breathing in psychosomatic, anxiety, or stress disorders and many medical disorders, and I believe that I am beginning to understand the role that it plays in them. I have learned that many of these conditions can be controlled when breathing retraining is incorporated in treatment strategies.

Much of what we know about breathing comes from yoga. There are many forms of yoga, but in general they are exercises that produce a particular state of profound muscle relaxation accompanied by a passive mental attitude. Most persons are familiar with transcendental meditation (TM). TM is a yoga technique thought to cause the practitioner to transcend, or rise beyond, conventional consciousness and reality, and to achieve a higher form of enlightenment. All forms of yoga involve breathing in one way or another. In some forms of yoga, breathing results from the exercises, while in other forms, breathing is guided to produce the desired outcome. Even modern physical therapy texts now incorporate yoga breathing, though they seldom acknowledge their debt to that venerable ancient practice.

Many of my clients have been told by their physician, at one time or another, "It's all in your mind," and "It's only an emotional problem." As for their breathing, in the absence of lung disease, it is common practice in conventional medicine to view it as the hysterical part of their general folly. "Stop hyperventilating," or "Here, breathe into this paper bag" are common clinical advice given clients showing stress. These were reported to me by persons who were referred to me for breathing retraining.

Disordered breathing is likely to be the best indication of stress and anxiety, for whatever reason. It is part of the mechanisms that rouse you to action in an emergency. It is also part of the mechanisms that rouse you to excitement and pleasure. In short, it reflects many of the body's life adjustment functions.

Abnormal breathing may have an emotional or a physical basis. Fear and sadness can cause breathing changes, but so can hypertension, kidney disease, and diabetes, just to mention a few factors. So do get checked up, but consider the breathing exercises I'll show you later in this book.

This book aims to describe the most common ways that breathing interacts with stress, emotional, psychological, and psychosomatic disorders, and to teach you a new and powerful technique that I developed that you can use yourself to reduce your discomfort, suffering, or pain.

  If, however, you are symptom free and you wish to improve your breath control, this breathing technique will help you to correct shallow breathing or other breathing difficulties. It will also help you to develop better breathing for exercise, and better breath control if you are a vocalist.

CHAPTER 2

The Hows and Whys
of Breathing

Breathing and Health

Susan is a college student. She hopes to enter law school in the fall. Before her frequent exams, she gets tense and anxious. Sometimes, she even has difficulty focusing her attention on the task before her. Her hands get cold and clammy and she reports that she has great difficulty catching her breath. Her breathlessness is particularly troublesome to her, and she just can't understand why it should be such a problem for her.

Susan, like most people, knows little about breathing. Most people think that breathing is just a "natural act." So why is it always affected by all these distractions? Most people don't have the slightest idea about how breathing works, and it needs to be explained to them.

To begin with, we thoroughly identify breathing with life, don't we? The Book of Genesis tells us: "And the Lord God formed man of the dust of the ground and breathed into his nostrils the breath of life; and the man became a living being." In Western tradition, all life begins with breath.

It is also perceived to end that way. In the New Testament, "Jesus, crying with a loud voice, said, 'Father into thy hands I commit my spirit!' And having said this he breathed his last." Breath is essentially on loan to us; we must return it when we are done with it.

The Upanishads represent Indian religious ideas and beliefs. The older of these go back to about 800 C.E. The Prasna Upanishad is based on the search for the Supreme Spirit, Brahman, by devout students who seek guidance from the sage, Pippalada.

According to tradition, the latter offered to answer the students' questions if they agreed to study with him for one year. At the end of that time, one of their number, Kabandi Katyayana, asked the sage the first of six questions: "Master, whence came all created things?" The sage answered: "In the beginning, the Creator longed for the joy of creation. He remained in meditation, and then came Rayi, matter, and Prana, life. These two, thought he, will produce beings for me."

Prana is the basic force of life. We are said to interact with or acquire this force through meditation, a process in which breathing plays a significant and sometimes crucial role. In the second part of the Svetasvatara Upanishad, Savitri, the God of Inspiration, instructs us: ". . . and when the body is silent steadiness, breathe rhythmically, through the nostrils with a peaceful ebbing and flowing of breath . . ."

Zen was introduced in China in the sixth century C.E. Less a religion than a tradition, it focuses on meditation to realize one's true nature. The first four of the "112 ways" are breathing instructions.

In the Chinese tradition, Qi (pronounced *chi*), a tripartite entity with both organic and inorganic properties, is the vital energy of life. Its third component, natural air Qi, is absorbed by the lungs from the air we breathe.

In the Western tradition, common metaphors also arouse our interest in breathing because they reflect our equating breathing with emotions and other passions of life, such as love, anger, joy, and sorrow.

We cherish the belief that each human feeling has a specific breathing pattern with which it is associated, and that we can identify that emotion by observing a person's breathing. Shakespeare, for instance, illustrated regret this way in Sonnet XXX:

When to the sessions of sweet silent thought
I summon up remembrance of things past,
I sigh the lack of many a thing I sought
And with old woes new wail my dear time's waste.

Tolstoy, in describing anger, wrote, "His pen is breathing re-
venge." Thomas Hood, in *The Bridge of Sighs*, tells us that

One more unfortunate,
Weary of breath,
Rashly importunate,
Gone to her death.

This morbid poem contrasts with Sir Walter Scott's well-known
patriotic and altruistic paean:

Breathes there the man, with soul so dead
Who never to himself hath said,
This is my own, my native land.

How Do You Breathe?

Here is a simple test: Are you wearing comfortable clothing that
does not confine you or restrict your breathing? Good. Now sit
comfortably back in your chair, preferably but not necessarily, in
front of a mirror.

Place your left hand on your chest, over your heart, and place
your right hand on your abdomen, over your belly button. Now pay
attention to your breathing. Note what each hand is doing as you
are breathing in, and as you are breathing out.

If both hands are rising and falling more or less simultaneously in
a shallow motion as you breathe, you are *chest-breathing*. If your abdomen moves in and your chest moves up when you inhale, and the
opposite happens when you exhale, you are *reverse-breathing*.

Ordinarily, you cannot count your breaths accurately when you
focus on them, because that changes them. But try anyway. If you
count over fourteen breaths per minute (b/min), you are probably
breathing too rapidly for someone who is sitting comfortably in a

chair. If the hand on your chest is virtually still, and the hand on your abdomen moves out when you inhale and moves in when you exhale, you are breathing correctly.

But isn't breathing automatic? How can there be so many different ways to breathe—some of them even alleged to be associated with stress-related disorders?

The Science of Respiration

Ordinarily, regulation of life functions is automatic. Breathing takes place without your thinking about it. The heart beats, blood is oxygenated and circulated, pressure is regulated, and waste gases are removed, all without requiring your attention.

Metabolism goes on without your attention, and so does the removal of various waste products. Many different parts of your body that wear down may be repaired or replaced as required: blood cells, stomach lining, and skin tissue, among others. Your hair and nails grow. Various segments of your nervous system automatically maintain you in the upright position and keep you informed about inside and outside temperature and environmental changes. Tissue water concentration is automatically regulated by kidney hormones.

In order to perform these remarkably complex functions, your body relies on an inherited, prewired program of reflexes that rely on various sensors to report what is happening at a particular body location. These may be sense organs such as those for vision, hearing, smell, and touch, or the carotid sinus or aortic arch mechanisms that respond to blood pressure (baroreceptors). There are also chemoreceptors that respond to concentrations of various chemicals, including gases such as oxygen and carbon dioxide.

Maintaining the proper concentration of oxygen and carbon dioxide is crucial because life fails rapidly without oxygen, but you will become ill, and you may eventually die, if the body does not maintain the proper concentration of carbon dioxide as well.

One cardinal rule in biological science is that unless it is interfered with, your body knows exactly what it is doing, and it always does the best thing to do under the circumstances. Consequently, if you have a disorder, you may reasonably assume that the disorder itself is the body's best adjustment to its present needs.

Contrary to what you may think, your body may not have let you down. The disorder may be evidence that your body is doing the best it can with what is available. It makes sense, therefore, to ask, "What do I have to do to make it unnecessary for my body to have to make this particular adjustment we call a disorder?"

Breathing is the only automatic vital life function we can voluntarily control, and therefore we can cause it to malfunction.

Ordinarily, breathing is under the control of reflexes that respond to information from various sensors located in different parts of the body, analyzing blood concentration of oxygen and carbon dioxide, reflexes of the lungs, and brain mechanisms. All of these mechanisms are subject to the influence of the automatic, or autonomic, nervous system, which adjusts body functions to expected or actual physical activity.

Information from the brain, relayed by the two branches of that autonomic nervous system, adjusts our bodies to meet environmental demands. The sympathetic branch of the autonomic nervous system commonly orders the release of an action hormone, noradrenaline, into the bloodstream and the acceleration of other action-related functions. It is the sympathetic branch that accelerates the heart, constricts arteries, increases blood circulation in the skin, and promotes sweating when we run, for instance. It is the parasympathetic branch that restores the physiological balance for energy conservation by returning all the accelerated functions back to normal levels.

Only in breathing can all of these automatic control mechanisms be readily bypassed. Within limits, we can increase respiration rate at will, or hold our breath pretty much regardless of what the circumstances dictate. But we cannot increase or decrease blood pressure at will, for instance, or speed up or slow digestion or sweating.

We can actually interfere with metabolism. Bear in mind that when we do this, the body has to adjust other processes so that the system is compensated, balanced, or in homeostasis.

All body functions are breathing-related, and they interact in complex ways. It is helpful to know a little bit about the process of breathing. Breathing is performed by the respiratory system, comprising the mouth and the nose and other airway passages, the muscles of the chest and rib cage, the diaphragm, and the lungs.

Body ventilation requires all of the above systems plus the circulatory system, including the heart and the interconnecting arteries and veins, to transport oxygen to the tissues and to remove carbon dioxide.

The Airway Passages to the Lungs

Contraction of the diaphragm and expansion of the rib cage result in a partial vacuum in the chest which causes air to be drawn into the respiratory system through the nose and mouth and into the lungs via the trachea, the bronchi, and bronchioles. Figure 1 illustrates the airways and the lungs.

Ideally, you should breathe through the nose because that prepares or conditions the air for the lungs. The nose, unlike the mouth, which is simply an opening designed to lead to the stomach, is better suited to respiration.

The nose accomplishes this important cleaning and conditioning process with its various structures. Two cavities leading from the trachea communicate with the outside world through the nostrils. The cavities are separated by a wall, the septum, and lined with a mucous blanket and hairs that act as a filtering system.

There is a small bulblike structure (turbinate) at the upper end of each nasal cavity that narrows the air passage to the trachea. Air drawn through the nose, separated right and left, swirls through nasal hair and past these turbinates, causing the formation of swirling currents that encourage the air filtration process by promoting the removal of coarser airborne particles. Smaller particles, as well as germs, are deposited on the sticky mucous blanket, to which they

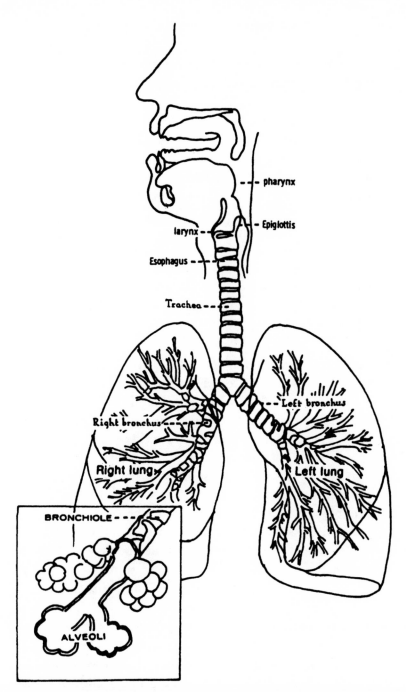

Figure 1 The pulmonary airways and the lungs. The inset shows the alveoli at the end of the airways where oxygen is exchanged for carbon dioxide.

adhere. Thus the nose helps to filter pollutants from the air before conducting it to the lungs.

Inspired air is also moisturized and warmed in the nose. As expired air rushes out past the turbinates, it meets the cooler air in the nose and deposits moisture on the mucous blanket of the turbinates. As inspired air swirls in past the turbinates, it picks up the now-warmed moisture previously deposited on the mucous blanket of the turbinates and returns it to the lungs, thus conserving body water. You can see now that the emphasis placed on breathing through the nose, encountered in most forms of yoga, was intuitively discovered long before the very essential functions of the nose in healthful breathing was scientifically determined.

Furthermore, air entering the body is rapidly warmed as it swirls past the turbinates. Even air entering the nose at a temperature of 45°F will reach body temperature by the time it has passed the turbinates.

The mucous membrane lining the nasal cavity, as well as the trachea, extends all the way down to the bronchi of the lungs. This lining is populated with cells from which little hairlike structures called *cilia* protrude. These cilia are constantly in motion, moving the mucous blanket up from the lungs, against gravity.

The mucous blanket has the capability to trap debris and bacteria, which it can destroy, removing these from the respiratory tract—usually by transport to the stomach.

The little blood vessels in the mucous lining of the nose also help in disinfecting its mucous blanket, by virtue of their rich supply of white blood cells, which are part of the body's immune system. However, the nose also has been shown to have an equally rich supply of infectious germs, including dangerous staphylococcus.

In addition to accommodating the sense of smell, the nose performs a vital function in correct breathing and may reflect various conditions of the body. Under the influence of increased levels of histamine released by the body as a reaction to allergy, the nasal mucous lining will swell and excrete fluid. That's what happens when you have a cold or hay fever.

The nasal lining will also swell under other conditions, including migraine and sexual arousal. For that reason, sexual arousal makes some persons sneeze; its sustained form results in a painful nasal congestion called "honeymoon nose." We are told that this condition may be readily remedied without medical intervention.

Inspired air enters the lungs through the trachea, a flexible tube made predominantly of cartilage, which divides into the bronchi, which in turn divide into smaller bronchioles, and again into alveolar ducts, which lead to the alveoli of the lungs.

The Lungs

Your lungs are made of porous tissue forming four lobes, two overlapping each other on each side of the chest, and lying more or less freely in the chest cavity while resting on the diaphragm. The chest cavity and associated rib-cage muscles are flexible up to a point, and can expand during chest breathing.

The lungs are covered by membranes (pleura) and constantly moistened by a soaplike lubricant (surfactant). This lubricant reduces friction as the lobes of the lungs expand and contract, and ride over each other during inspiration and expiration.

Atmospheric air finds its way, via the air passages, to the alveoli, extremely small spherical sacs in the lungs, where the oxygen and carbon dioxide gas exchange takes place. Small vents connect adjacent alveoli.

There, atmospheric air is separated from the returning oxygen-depleted blood in small blood vessels by a set of thin membranes. There is an enormous number of alveoli in the lungs; their surface area, if they were unfolded in an adult man, would be about seventy-five square meters.

Alveoli form small clusters, like grapes (after which they are named), each with its own blood circulation. Oxygen dissolves through the membranes in the capillaries into the blood, and carbon dioxide passes from the blood into the alveoli until the pressure of the two gases is equal in the blood and in the alveolar air. This gas exchange and equalization process occurs rapidly and continuously.

Then blood, stripped of its excess carbon dioxide and oxygenated, is ready for the return trip to body tissues via the heart.

Tidal Volume and Breathing Rate

The volume of air entering and leaving the lungs with each inspiration and expiration cycle is called the tidal volume. The minute-ventilation of the lungs is the tidal volume per minute. Changes in minute-volume almost always reflect changes in metabolism in a healthy individual. High minute-volume reflects increased activity such as running, while low minute-volume reflects a low level of activity such as rest.

In a healthy individual, breathing rate usually follows minute-volume. Rapid breathing accompanies a high minute-volume, while slower breathing goes with a lower minute-volume.

In a healthy individual, this relationship between minute-volume and breathing rate is closely regulated by the level of metabolic activity. The relationship is so well known that when minute-volume and breathing rate are out of step, we know that the individual is in some sort of trouble: it could be a metabolic disorder, lung disease, or another condition, but it spells trouble.

That's why, as you will see, inexplicably rapid or slow breathing, or high or low minute-volume, can indicate trouble and can also cause it. Inexplicably high or low breathing rate and minute-volume tell us that the body is compensating for something unusual going on. Such an event is always accompanied by loss of heart-breath rhythm.

Atmospheric air entering the lungs contains about 21 percent oxygen, 0.03 percent (3/10 of 1 percent) carbon dioxide, 78 percent nitrogen, and varying quantities of water vapor, other gases such as carbon monoxide, methane, helium, argon, neon, and pollutants.

The volume of air leaving the lungs in the expiration cycle of breathing, the end-tidal volume, holds about 5 percent carbon dioxide. As you will see, that carbon dioxide level is crucial, and it tells us a great deal about what the body is doing.

In fact, it is rarely the oxygen level, but usually the carbon dioxide level, that will be found to be abnormal in most of the conditions that affect you. You will see that it is sensible that the breathing technique described in this book features a way of making sure that the carbon dioxide level remains normal—not too high, not too low.

Normal and Abnormal Breathing

Our principal concern in this book will be how to breathe so as to best bring minute-volume and carbon dioxide levels back to normal. If we can regulate those, blood will flow normally through the circulatory system, and ample oxygen will be available to all body tissues. I should add here that it has been recently discovered that there is yet a third gas crucially important to our life functions. It is nitric oxide. More about nitric oxide later.

We call lack of oxygen *anoxia*, reduced oxygenation of body tissues, *hypoxia*. Chronic hypoxia is called *hypoxemia*. None of these conditions is desirable. In fact, they are so undesirable that many of us do aerobic exercises to avoid them. Aerobic exercise contributes more oxygen to the body than is required by the ongoing activity. In a sense, it creates an oxygen surplus.

When you are sitting quietly, you should breathe about twelve breaths per minute (b/min). In a normal man at rest, tidal volume is about 500 milliliters. Twelve times tidal volume, or 6,000 milliliters, is equal to minute-volume. End-tidal carbon dioxide will be about 4.5 percent to 5.0 percent. On average, men breathe a little slower than women, but not very much.

Most persons with normal metabolism who nevertheless breathe more rapidly than normal will raise minute-volume and expel excess carbon dioxide.

Since tidal volume and breathing frequency are ordinarily coupled, neither can vary independently. If you breathe quickly, your breaths must become shallow. If you take shallow breaths, you will have to breathe more quickly. However, in a person with a breathing disorder due to lung or metabolic disease, that relationship may become uncoupled. One can find slow breathing and shallow volume in some lung diseases, and one can also observe rapid breathing with exaggerated volume in some metabolic disorders.

Stress and the Diaphragm

We also find that most persons who are at rest, and who are free of metabolic or lung diseases, may also have shallow breathing simply from the partial contraction of the diaphragm that comes from their stress reaction to the demands of their world. This partial diaphragm contraction can limit the volume of air taken in with each breath. Since metabolic demand requires a more or less constant minute-volume, their breathing will quicken.

The partial contraction of the diaphragm is part of the pattern of muscle tension in a stress response, and it reduces the space in the chest into which the lungs can expand during the inspiration phase of breathing. With reduced lung expansion, the average person will tend to increase breathing rate to attempt to maintain a more or less constant minute-volume. This is a hyperventilation compensatory mechanism.

Once upon a time, I am told (for I am not *that* old), women wore corsets that squeezed their midriff. These corsets were laced up the back, and it gave them a sort of hourglass figure much admired then. It was not uncommon that they would occasionally develop a dizziness and faintness then called the "vapors." The corset would be loosened, and the vapors attributed to feminine hysteria. Today we know that the vapors resulted from hyperventilation caused by restriction of the excursion of the diaphragm. These women couldn't get enough air with each breath, so they had to breathe faster. In so doing, they lost too much carbon dioxide.

The body's attempt to maintain more or less constant minute-volume by more rapid breathing in the face of low, shallow breaths may result in an excessive loss of carbon dioxide, affecting the body's acid-base balance. That acid-base balance is crucial to normal life. The body is absolutely intolerant of shifts in the acid-base balance.

A substance can be neutral, that is, neither acidic nor base. But, the body works hard to maintain the blood at a slight degree of alkalinity. When blood alkalinity rises above that normal level, the condition is called alkalosis. Whereas when alkalinity decreases somewhat below normal level, we call it acidosis because it is less alkaline. But, normally blood is not really acidic. Profound acidosis is a life-threatening condition sometimes encountered in kidney disease or diabetes, to mention just a few examples. Hyperventilation causes alkalosis. An increase in the acidity of blood can be lethal, and both the kidneys and the lungs work overtime to try to avoid that. The kidneys excrete acid, and the lungs expel more carbon dioxide, also helping to excrete acid. The lungs, however, carry the lion's share of that responsibility (85 percent), while the kidneys do about 15 percent of the job.

The body has some buffers, but the kidney/lung mechanism is crucial to its proper functioning. Metabolism in each cell in your body is highly dependent on the right acid-base balance. Even small shifts to acidic, or to alkaline, create enormous problems for your body cells. Alkalosis causes the blood to retain some oxygen instead of releasing it freely to the body tissues that need it. The body is slightly more tolerant to alkalosis than it is to acidosis. Therefore, "acidosis," here meaning reduced alkalinity, requires the kidneys to work overtime to correct the condition.

Hyperventilation invariably compensates for something in the body. It is not due to hysteria.

The Red Cell Hemoglobin Oxygen Magnet

Imagine that the hemoglobin molecules in your red blood cells function like tiny magnets. They can pick up or release oxygen. The degree of their "magnetism" depends on the acid-base balance. At the proper balance, they will pick up oxygen in the lungs and give it up at the tissues where the magnetic pull is greater because of the greater density of carbon dioxide, and therefore acidity.

In hyperventilation, so much carbon dioxide may be lost that blood becomes more alkaline (base) than it should be, and the magnetism of the hemoglobin molecules increases so that it may give up less oxygen to the tissues as it makes the rounds.

We have recently discovered that certain cells in your body produce the gas nitric oxide. Nitric oxide causes blood vessels to relax. The lungs also make nitric oxide, and the hemoglobin in your red blood cells absorbs it and ferries it around just as it does oxygen and carbon dioxide. It is released in your small blood vessels, arterioles, and capillaries, where it enhances blood circulation to counteract the fact that hemoglobin arriving there saturated with oxygen tends to narrow blood vessels by causing them to constrict.

Breathing Mode: Chest Versus Abdominal

There is also a breathing mode: chest (thoracic) versus abdominal (diaphragmatic). In chest breathing, the rib cage spreads slightly and the chest rises dramatically. Most persons don't realize that the chest cannot expand by the action of its muscles. Muscles can only contract. What appears to be an enlargement of the chest is really its rising as it is pulled upward by muscles in the neck and at the base of the skull (scalenes).

In spite of its dramatic appearance, this breathing mode results in relatively little air entering the lungs. On the other hand, abdominal/ diaphragmatic breathing, accomplished by alternately contracting the diaphragm and abdominal muscles, increases the space in the chest into which the lungs can expand to accept air. A far greater volume of air is exchanged with abdominal breathing than with chest breathing.

Breathing also has rhythm, the relative duration of the pattern of inspiration and expiration as these are repeated over time. This is usually called the *I/E ratio*. In deep diaphragmatic breathing, inspiration and expiration are equal in duration. But more typically, one of the phases of breathing—inspiration or expiration—may be found to be exaggerated or too brief.

Ideally, in a person at rest, diaphragmatic breathing (through the nose only) should prevail at a rate of only three to five breaths per minute, with proportional increase in tidal volume so that minute-volume will be about normal. The I/E ratio will be about 1:00. In other words, the duration of inhale is about the same as exhale.

Most individuals at rest, and without regard to the actual mechanics of their breathing, ordinarily breathe at about twelve to fifteen breaths per minute (b/min). Naturally, as activity increases, breathing rate as well as minute-volume will rise.

In abdominal breathing, ventilation of the lungs is accomplished in this way: Contraction of the diaphragm creates a partial vacuum in the space between the lungs and the rib cage. The lungs expand into that space while filling with air. The contraction of the diaphragm above, and somewhat behind, the viscera pushes them forward, making the abdomen move forward. This perceived motion of the abdomen is the reason for calling diaphragmatic breathing "abdominal breathing" or "belly breathing." It should be noted that no air ever enters the abdomen proper.

When the lungs are filled, the distended abdominal muscles contract again, causing the viscera to push the diaphragm back into its original place. This squeezes the lungs, expelling the air in expiration.

As activity level increases, other components are added to the breathing process, including "chest expansion"—actually the chest rising.

Chest breathing is accomplished mostly by raising the rib cage. It is an inefficient form of breathing because the volume of air entering and leaving the lungs is considerably less than that in diaphragmatic breathing. Consequently, chest breathers must breathe more rapidly in order to maintain an adequate minute-volume.

With their increased respiration rate, chest breathers are likely candidates for hyperventilation because they will expel more than the normal amount of carbon dioxide from their body.

Why do people develop chest breathing? Clearly, they must develop it because diaphragmatic breathing is the way we all breathed originally as infants. There are many reasons; some are basically indications that there is something wrong with the body.

There may be pulmonary problems due to diseases of the lungs. Anything that interferes with air entering or leaving the lungs, interferes with the gas exchange in the alveoli, or interferes with blood circulation through the lungs will cause changes in breathing rate and pattern and may result in additional problems created by the resultant hyperventilation.

There may be metabolic disorders whose compensatory mechanisms involve breathing. Hypoglycemia, diabetes, heart disease, and diseases of the kidneys or liver may result in *metabolic acidosis*. This means that your body's acid-base balance has shifted toward greater acidity and must be compensated for by more rapid breathing.

Other physical conditions will alter breathing, including disorders of the respiratory centers in the brain, metabolic problems relating to pituitary, adrenal, or thyroid function, and various forms of anemia.

Emotional stress and psychological disorders constitute yet another category of known contributors to dysrhythmic and disordered breathing due to adaptations that may entail breath holding or unusual shifts to shallow chest breathing.

There is another source of unusual breathing—adherence to fashion in clothing and the desire to appear thin. Although we no longer favor the pinched-waist look, we sometimes squeeze into clothes that are too tight for us, causing the designer clothes syndrome.

This by no means exhausts the list, but should give you an indication of the variety of different reasons why you may wind up with disordered breathing. Because of the very real possibility that hyperventilation may compensate for metabolic acidosis, as in diabetes, giving a paper bag for re-breathing to someone who is observed to hyperventilate may be hazardous unless the medical history of that person is known to you. Don't do it!

CHAPTER 3

The Hyperventilation Syndrome

When You're Told Your
Disorder Is All in Your Head

Karen is a thirty-year-old special-ed schoolteacher who has a very demanding job. She works with a class of learning-impaired and sometimes emotionally troubled fifth graders. She has, for some years, been routinely afflicted with headaches. The many physicians she consulted, as time went on, could find no medical basis for them and so, in concert with her difficult job, she was told that the headaches were probably a stress-related or psychosomatic disorder. She was recommended over-the-counter analgesics whenever she experienced headaches, and she was also counseled to see a psychotherapist.

The term *psychosomatic* is somewhat outdated now and seldom heard. There is a substitute term, *psychophysiological*. The term psychosomatic is derived from the psychoanalytic theory that many disturbing symptoms and conditions are really physical manifestations of underlying psychological conflict. A more modern approach recognizes that this is not the case, that distressed mental states cannot cause a physical disorder, but can aggravate one to which an individual is predisposed.

31

For instance, stress does not cause headaches in those not so predisposed. But it can increase the frequency and severity of such attacks in those who are so predisposed.

Family history is often a clue to predisposition. You tend to inherit it. If there is no family history of headaches, it is not likely that your stress will cause one. But is there a family history of allergies, of asthma, of gastritis?

The Psychoanalytic Theory of Psychosomatic Disorders

Psychiatrists used to think that Freud's theories explained how the mind could cause symptoms. Freud held that psychosomatic symptoms are the physical expressions of sexual conflicts or of unexpressed anger. Accordingly, psychosomatic symptoms should be specific to unconscious emotional conflicts.

Symptoms with no discernible cause were taken as evidence that you were suffering from hysteria, which is what you were said to have if you had symptoms with no discernible cause. Thus, persons were said to have hysterical this, that, and the other if no cause could be found.

Hypertension was thought to be related to repressed hostility, while asthma was held to be the expression of an unuttered appeal for parental love and attention.

According to more modern views, the requirements of living in a family and in a community, getting along with others on the job, and so on, may be stressors that contribute to illness. The price we pay for controlling social interactions may have a nonspecific weakening effect on the body's ability to protect itself from diseases. Here are some additional theories.

Walter B. Cannon was a noted American physiologist who postulated that emotions are the result of a sudden, involuntary, physiological adjustment of the autonomic nervous system to the requirements of survival in a crisis situation.

The autonomic nervous system has two main branches: the sympathetic branch, which arouses us to action, and the parasympathetic branch, which returns us to a preaction state.

The autonomic nervous system is mostly under the control of a brain center, the hypothalamus, responsible for such processes as emotion, eating, drinking, and the sex drive. It automatically adjusts most of your involuntary biological life functions. But it is also affected by the frontal lobes of the brain where thinking takes place, and thus it is influenced by thinking.

The sympathetic branch of the autonomic nervous system also orients us to environmental changes, some of which may herald danger. This invariably begins with breath holding and is followed closely by the release of action hormones (adrenaline and noradrenaline) into the bloodstream, raising blood pressure and heart rate and causing extensive skeletal muscular tension and blood circulation adjustments, as well as involuntary changes in digestive and other internal organs.

Pavlovian physiologists who studied the way that these autonomic nervous system adjustments of the body could become conditioned to any environmental stimuli came to the conclusion that merely eliciting them, for whatever reason, could in itself be stressful.

Some years ago I was sitting in the shade of an umbrella at a sidewalk cafe in San Francisco sipping a tall glass of ginger ale. Two young women were sitting at a similar table nearby also enjoying refreshments. One of them had an infant in a stroller by her side and the other had a small child whose uncontrollable and unruly behavior marked him as a potential candidate for Ritalin.

The mother of this child turned to her friend in anguish and declared, "God, this boy gives me a headache!" This exclamation reminded me of Hans Selye's theory and, unthinking, a smile rose to my lips. Unfortunately, it was noticed and returned with a stone-cold glare.

Hans Selye was a Canadian Nobel laureate whose book, *Stress Without Distress*, summarized his now widely accepted theory of stress that combined the work of Cannon and of the Pavlovians. He put it this way:

> Mental tensions, frustrations, insecurity and aimlessness are among the
> most damaging stressors, and psychosomatic studies have shown how
> often they cause migraine headache, peptic ulcers, heart attacks, and
> hypertension.[1]

Selye thought that medical disorders were caused by stress, but
at least here is a departure from the belief that it is unconscious sexual conflicts that cause them. What he says basically is that you
were not designed to withstand prolonged tension, anger, and frus-
trations.

Rather, we seem to have been designed to function with efficiency, meaning minimal energy expenditure, unless otherwise indicated. But when survival requires it, we can rapidly muster, and
maintain, a high energy output to meet emergency demand in ef-
fecting a successful defense or escape from a threatening situation.
We are built essentially like a quarter horse. We can run fast, but not
long. One can be sure that this comes as no surprise to you as you
think about the things in life that you need to cope with.

Naturally, this increased arousal is automatically accomplished by
the sympathetic branch of the autonomic nervous system, and may
be observed as vigilance, tension, anger, or rage. When the threat
subsides, the arousal dissipates because it becomes inhibited by the
opposing action of the parasympathetic branch of the autonomic
nervous system. This readjustment to prearousal energy expenditure
was termed *homeostasis* by Cannon.

What happens if you continue the energy-costly sympathetic
arousal state is explained by Selye in this way:

> ... animals exposed to continuous stress for long periods go through the
> three phases of the GAS [General Adaptation Syndrome]: the initial
> alarm reaction, followed by resistance and, eventually, exhaustion.[2]

A particular stressful event may result in nonspecific physical effects in addition to specific ones. The combination, if it becomes
chronic, may result in a symptom.

As you can see, according to this theory, there really is no rational reason why a symbolic relationship should be thought to link the

symptoms to the stressors. In fact, there is not even a basis for a rational guess as to the source of stress, given the symptoms.

You may of course wonder why Selye, or anyone else, would think that obviously adaptive mechanisms—the very same mechanisms that keep us alive—would cause stress and ultimately result in symptoms.

Some blame failed evolution: no new behaviors have evolved to deal with trains that do not keep to schedules; unrealistic work demands; family or marital discord; screaming or whining children; health or financial concerns; interpersonal workplace conflicts; sedentary daily routine; fear of technology, computers, and modernization; fear of aging and loss of social status; and so on.

And so our tendency is to respond to modern threats in the same way that our primitive ancestors might have done hundreds of thousands of years ago: we can gasp, tense, snarl, lash out, run. But because these automatic reactions threaten others, we quickly learn to hide them with voluntary cover-up actions: we refrain, wherever possible, from showing frustration, anger, fear, and pain—and even joy, love, and pleasure. The consequence of this strategy may be that the unseen reactions, such as breath holding, increased pulse rate and blood pressure, and dry throat, persist.

That young mother did not know that her anger and frustration could be dramatically reduced by lowering her arousal level with a few diaphragmatic breaths.

I often ask my classes to perform the following experiment: "Now class, I want you all to close your eyes. Okay, now, in your mind's eye, try to picture a lemon and at the same time say the word 'lemon' to yourself silently. Now, open your eyes. Good! How many of you could do this without salivating? Raise your hand if you could." Few hands rise.

The reflex, automatic action of the body, such as withdrawing a finger when touching an unprotected electric wire, is different from automatically salivating when you hear or see the word "lemon." The first reaction is unconditional. It does not depend on learning.

In the second case, a person would not respond by salivating if s/he had never experienced a lemon.

The process whereby anything becomes capable of reliably producing an automatic or reflex response is called *conditioning*.

There are different ways in which we become conditioned. If you were the child of overprotective parents, it is likely that the chance discovery that you can avoid school by feigning illness would increase in frequency with each successfully faked episode. Here we see the operation of the rewards, avoiding school and getting parental attention, that follow a voluntary behavior, faking illness. This is also conditioning. It is called *operant conditioning*.

It may well be that no theory fits the facts and that all disorders really have multiple causes: it is frequently the case that the flu is "going around," and that some people get it while others don't. Why is that? One explanation is that stress, or emotional state, affects the body's immune system, impairing the ability to fight off invading viruses or bacteria.

The idea that there is a cause-effect relationship between emotions and illness is not exactly new. But the question of which is cause and which is effect has been debated for some time. For instance, as long ago as the 1890s, W. F. Evans wrote in his book, *Mental Medicine*, that:

> Many physicians of extensive experience are destitute of the ability of searching out the mental causes of disease; they cannot read the book of the heart, and yet it is in this book that are inscribed, day by day, and hour by hour, all the griefs, and all the miseries, and all the vanities, and all the fears, and all the joys, and all the hopes of man, and in which will be found the most active and incessant principle of that frightful series of organic changes which constitute pathology.[3]

Pavlov preferred a purely physiological explanation which has greatly influenced modern medicine:

> My attitude towards the psychiatric material, however, differed greatly from the usual attitude of specialists. . . . I always reasoned on a purely physiological basis and constantly explained to myself the Psychical activity of the patients in definite physiological terms.[4]

Stress and Disease

In 1967, two researchers, Doctors Holmes and Rahe, concluded that there is a strong relationship between selected "life events" and illness. Their study, based on more than five thousand patients, supported a widely held belief that stressful life events are an important contribution to the onset of disease—not only psychosomatic disorders, but infectious diseases and injuries as well. And so they devised a *social readjustment rating scale*, which accords numerical values to various common events in ordinary people's lives.

To use this scale, one simply checks off the items that one experienced within the past year, then he or she adds up the score. If one scores 300 or better, one would have a 90 percent chance of developing an illness; with a score of 150, a 50-50 chance; and so on.

Though the occurrence of disease may require multiple predispositions, predisposition does not condemn you to illness. Preventive measures can be taken to avoid their effects, and we are beginning to learn much about them. One of the aims of this book is to alert you to a number of such factors, and thereby help you to overcome many of them.

In the *Handbook of Behavioral Medicine,*[5] Doctors Krantz and Glass report that on the basis of the study of the physiological effect of emotions, it is now generally held that personality traits, coping dispositions, or other personality factors could influence the development and course of disease.

What Does Stress Do to Me?

Practitioners recognize the psychophysiological basis of many diseases and disorders. A composite of the index of contemporary medical books yields the following list:

- adrenal disease (Addison's disease, Cushing's syndrome)
- allergy
- amenorrhea (irregular menstrual periods)
- anorexia

- arthritis
- backache
- bronchial asthma
- cancer
- cardiac arrhythmia
- cardiovascular disease
- colds
- Crohn's disease (chronic inflammatory bowel disease)
- dermatitis
- diabetes
- duodenal ulcers
- epilepsy
- Epstein-Barr virus (mononucleosis)
- gastrointestinal pathology
- Graves' disease (hyperthyroidism)
- headache
- herpes virus
- hives
- hypertension
- lupus erythematosus
- migraine
- myositis (lumbago)
- pain
- peptic ulcers
- Raynaud's disease
- rheumatoid arthritis
- sexual organ dysfunction
- suppression of immune response
- ulcerative colitis
- urethritis (bacterial and chronic yeast)

This impressive list is still by no means exhaustive, but it covers most of the things that you are likely to have heard of. Most remarkably, none of the major textbooks include the hyperventilation syndrome (HVS), which a number of prominent psychiatrists still attribute to hysteria to this day.

These disorders are not imaginary. You are not malingering if you suffer from one of them. They frequently even "run in families."

Do you recognize any of them? Do you suffer from any of them? If you do, you are in excellent company. Let's look at a particular case.

Margaret: Every Symptom in the Book

Margaret is a twenty-seven-year-old divorced administrative assistant. She is of medium height, on the slim side, and well groomed. She has no children.

She reported experiencing headaches, muscle tension, chest pain, and "skipped beats," in addition to bloating and occasional sleeplessness. These symptoms began several years ago, apparently unconnected to any particular event in her life. Then they gradually worsened: headaches became more frequent, and more intense, and she dreaded the skipped heartbeats.

When she first entered my office, I noted that her handshake was limp, her hand was cold and clammy, and her posture had a "droop," suggesting depression.

She related having seen numerous physicians who told her that she was fine. Her cardiac arrhythmia (ventricular premature contractions), which she perceived as skipped beats, was not thought to be dangerous, and her problems were said to be emotional. She was advised to seek proper psychiatric help.

She reported every symptom in the book: shortness of breath, dizziness, dry throat and frequent swallowing, blurred vision, faintness, chest pain, heart palpitations and skipped beats, muscle aches, pain, cramps and twitches, sweating, frequent headaches, chronic indigestion and gas, cold extremities, a fear of dying or going crazy, depression, and chronic tiredness.

Her blood pressure was near normal, but her pulse was slightly elevated. Her breathing was a shallow and rapid twenty-six breaths per minute (almost twice the normal rate).

Analysis of her breathing pattern with a special instrument called a capnometer, which analyzes the carbon dioxide level in exhaled (end-tidal) breath, showed a low carbon dioxide level (a typical normal level averages about 5 percent). And her hands were exceptionally cold. The left index finger temperature was an uncommonly low 76°F (three degrees above room temperature). The normal expected value is about 87 to 90°F.

What does this tell us about Margaret? Her rapid breathing is due to the shallowness of her breaths, as is common in anxiety and tension patterns with the diaphragm more or less "frozen." Cold hands result from constricted blood vessels due to low blood carbon dioxide.

Here is a case where numerous disparate symptoms, none clearly evidence of a medical disease, were attributed entirely to psychological factors. But stop and think for a moment: If you've never had a skipped beat, would you know what it is? Could you produce one? How can one imagine that the mind produces symptoms?

Why Hasn't Anything Worked for Me So Far?

Over the past fifty years, highly respected medical publications have reported that certain kinds of mental and physical disorders are associated with common breathing irregularities, especially hyperventilation. Breathing retraining can control them quickly and at little or no cost.

In your search for relief you may have consulted numerous doctors and obeyed their instructions faithfully. You probably watch your diet, do aerobic exercises, and consume quantities of various medications. Yet you seem to be treatment proof. In fact, some among you may be what Dr. L. C. Lum, noted British lung specialist, calls "the patient with the fat [medical] folder syndrome."

It has perhaps been suggested to you that you may be sabotaging otherwise miraculous treatments and you may blame yourself for their failure and wonder what you are doing wrong. The gong has sounded the end of round 1. You sheepishly return to your corner wondering what to do next. Round 2 consists of sifting among self-help books.

Why are there so many of them on the market? Logic dictates that they must serve a very important purpose. Well, if the orthodox treatments work, why so many self-help books?

The preferred explanation is that many persons resist getting well. This is an old ploy that psychologists call *secondary gain*. You are thought to derive some sort of advantage from your disorder. If you don't benefit from treatment, it is because you are not motivated to get well, presumably because you derive some benefit from being ill.

It could be that there are some people who do not wish to get well. But the overwhelming majority of persons who suffer from stress-related disorders almost desperately do want to get well.

The basic message of this book is that stress reactions inevitably are the result of chronic physical "adjust" and "readjust" mechanisms of the autonomic nervous system that ultimately deprive the body of oxygen as it is burned up in these futile mini-emergencies. That is why an enlightened doctor may recommend exercise—aerobics.

Aerobic exercise increases the body's available oxygen and therefore promotes wellness: where it is not contraindicated because of disability, aerobic exercise promotes health and reduces health care costs.

Delivering oxygen to the body is the responsibility of the respiratory system. Breathing is the process by which air enters the bloodstream via the lungs. Proper breathing, and correcting common breathing disorders, is the ultimate form of aerobics.

The Hyperventilation Syndrome: A Sigh Is Not Just a Sigh

The knock on the door was so light it was almost imperceptible. Janet walked into my office and sat down in the chair which I pointed out to her. She appeared to be in her middle twenties and she was well groomed. She seemed tired and stoop-shouldered, and she did not look at me directly. For a moment, she sat quietly with her hands in her lap.

I looked at her and said to her: "Good afternoon Miss R., how are you today?"

She sighed noticeably and answered.

You movie aficionados, you remember the line from that famous song in the movie, *Casablanca*, "A kiss is just a kiss, a sigh is just a sigh." Well, a kiss may be just a kiss, but to this clinical respiratory physiologist, a sigh tells an entirely different story, and it can be a very disturbing one.

From the earliest scientific studies of breathing, those that date to the 1920s and 1930s, "sighing respiration" was taken as a signal for emotional disturbance. Before that time, it was thought that sighing respiration was a signature of heart disease because it was prominent in *effort syndrome*, which was thought to be a form of heart disease.

But it quickly became evident that it appeared only in heart patients who also had an anxiety disorder. Similar sighing respiration was subsequently also found in anxiety patients who had no history of heart disease.

Many years later, effort syndrome was recognized to be due to hyperventilation, a condition in which sighing is often prominent.

Under ordinary circumstances, when a person is not doing something that requires activity, breathing should be easy, even, slow, and deep. With increased activity, breathing rate goes up to meet the increased ventilation and metabolic demands of the body.

But in some persons, breathing is rapid even at rest. When this rapid breathing results in an excessive loss of carbon dioxide, it is said to be hyperventilation. Hyperventilation has been known for many years to be both the cause and the result of stress, emotional, and psychophysiological disorders.

The late Dr. H. E. Walker, clinical professor of psychiatry at New York University Medical School, wrote that hyperventilation is one of the most misunderstood and most frequently overlooked illnesses in medicine.[6] Even patients who obviously hyperventilate in the emergency room and subsequently undergo exhaustive and expensive cardiac and neurological workups often remain undiagnosed.

Why Do We Hyperventilate?

Hyperventilation may have an emotional basis. Fright, anxiety, panic disorder, agoraphobia, or other signs of emotion may lead to hyperventilation. Conversely, hyperventilation can also cause these conditions.

Sometimes, hyperventilation has a physical basis. As noted earlier, hyperventilation is present in all conditions in which the acid-base balance of the blood shifts toward acid.

The lungs play an important role in maintaining the acid-base balance of the blood. Any condition that increases acidity will cause you to breathe faster to expel more carbon dioxide from the lungs. Rapid breathing is prominent in many disorders that result in acidosis, including those of the heart and the kidneys, diabetes, and hypoglycemia.

Rarely, there may be a neurological basis to hyperventilation. A lesion in any of several brain centers, such as the pons, or medulla, may result in hyperventilation.

Few primary care physicians assess breathing in routine medical checkups, even in the United Kingdom, where it was recommended that they do so by a panel of medical experts. Consequently, we do not know how commonly hyperventilation is due to lung diseases such as chronic obstructive pulmonary disease (COPD), bronchial asthma, chronic bronchitis, and emphysema. There are other lung problems, which are in extraordinary cases due to fungi, molds, or parasitic infections, or to fibrosis or other conditions.

Hyperventilation has, paradoxically, also been linked to low blood pressure and fainting spells (*syncope*), to cardiac arrhythmias, and to epileptic seizures. This by no means exhausts the list, as you will see. Hyperventilation has been observed in an extraordinary number of psychological, psychiatric, and physical disorders. It is often impossible to tell if it is a cause or consequence.

The Effects of Hyperventilation

Hyperventilation unrelated to lung, heart, or other disease has the following medical characteristics: When a person breathes room air, arterial blood pH is above 7.4,[7] and the concentration of carbon dioxide in blood is below 4.0 percent.

Typically, hyperventilatory breathing shows increased minute-volume and rapid breathing. There often may be predominantly chest breathing, with chest heaving, and frequent sighing. The breathing pattern may be irregular, with unequal inspiration and expiration; and there may be spasms, gasps, or breathing interruption, or apnea.

Most persons will readily recognize the acute hyperventilation that may arise in frightful situations. But chronic hyperventilation is quite subtle and its effects may not invariably be obvious.

I sometimes find that clients who hyperventilate have rapid breathing, and sometimes grossly exaggerated chest movements. But more typically, breathing is very shallow—with almost imperceptible breathing movements—often accompanied by much sighing.

When some of the symptoms of hyperventilation syndrome, such as shallow breathing, frequent sighing, dizziness, a sense of unreality, or an inability to catch one's breath, are present in a person, but it is not clear that s/he is, in fact, hyperventilating, some clinicians employ a *hyperventilation challenge* procedure: the client is asked to breathe deeply and rapidly (twenty to thirty b/min) for about two to three minutes.

I am opposed to the use of this hyperventilation challenge, even though Professor Walker recommended it. I consider it hazardous: As blood levels of carbon dioxide decrease, arterial blood vessels throughout the body begin to constrict. There are countless medical reports that hyperventilation causes arterial blood vessels in the heart and in the brain to constrict, seriously impairing blood circulation to those organs.

Many years ago, Dr. Joshua Rosett showed that "overventilation," as he called hyperventilation, can lead to epileptic seizures.[8] More recently, Dr. L. C. Lum, a noted British pulmonary physician, cautioned against using hyperventilation as a diagnostic test in persons with chest pain or with neuromuscular disorders because, among other effects, it has been shown to trigger angina and arrhythmias.

Dr. Gottstein and colleagues, reporting on the brain, put it even more strongly when they said that hyperventilation in cases where the carbon dioxide concentration drops below 2.5 percent will cause an inadequate oxygen supply even in healthy subjects.[9] Clearly, this should be kept in mind when considering "therapeutic" hyperventilation.

Keep in mind that this cautionary technical note was a warning to professionals using the hyperventilation challenge that it may dangerously reduce oxygen to the heart and the brain.

Low blood levels of carbon dioxide is said to be a primary cause of ischemic heart disease, a condition of impaired blood supply to the heart. A comparable phenomenon, also related to low blood levels of carbon dioxide in the brain, has been linked to stroke, and to the so-called transient ischemic attacks (TIA).

Hyperventilation challenge is even used in some therapeutic situations *precisely* because it will trigger symptoms, and in others to show the person that the symptoms they experience are due to their hyperventilation. I prefer to make it a practice to simply tell my clients about the origin of their symptoms without requiring them to reexperience them just to prove a point. Then, I teach them how to breathe correctly.

I recommend that you determine if you are a chronic hyperventilator on the basis of the following signs proposed by Dr. L. C. Lum. You are hyperventilating if breathing is predominantly thoracic (chest); if little use is made of the diaphragm (abdominal movement is minimal); if breathing is punctuated by frequent sighs; if sighing has an effortless quality with a marked forward and upward movement of the sternum but little lateral expansion.[10]

By the way, persons who commonly breathe normally have difficulty imitating the chest-breathing movements used by those who usually hyperventilate.

Finally, as noted above, chronic hyperventilators frequently precede speech utterances with a deep sigh: they will sigh deeply even if you just ask them their name.

Hyperventilation is probably the most common of the so-called stress-related breathing disorders. There are varying reports of its frequency in the population at large, ranging between about 10 percent and 25 percent. It has been estimated to account for roughly 60 percent of emergency ambulance calls in major U.S. city hospitals.

Could My Symptoms Be
Hyperventilation-Related?

Doctors Kerr, Dalton, and Gliebe, pioneer clinical researchers, told us in the 1930s that critical social, moral, and economic changes in the world have resulted in an ever-increasing number of patients who are observed to have symptoms intimately associated with the struggle for security, for independence, or for whatever state is presumed to assure the spiritual and material happiness of the individual.

I relate this here to show you that the concerns of patients in the 1930s do not appear to be vastly different from yours today. Furthermore, that article, published in *Annals of Internal Medicine*, addresses symptoms reported by general medical practice patients and not psychiatric patients. It is a fairly recent development that "psychosomatic" symptoms are thought to be a medical concern.

Doctor Kerr and colleagues further assert that, while not seen exclusively among persons suffering from "neuroses," the symptoms of hyperventilation are frequently found in such persons, and that their manifestations are due to anxiety states. In other words, the symptoms essentially result from the interaction between emotional and physiological factors. This is a clear contradiction of the psychoanalytic theory then prevailing and is, in fact, an early statement consistent with the term "psychophysiological."

Now the question is, of course, "What happens to these persons who suffer from anxiety-related disorders?" According to Doctor Kerr and colleagues, patients with these symptoms "haunt the offices of physicians and specialists in every field of medical practice."

Here you may recognize the so-called hypochondriacs, whose complaints are invariably dismissed as being "all in your mind," and those whose identifiable physical symptoms are treated with sedatives, tranquilizers, and the admonition, "You have to take care of yourself! Relax!" You will be drawn to the altogether correct conclusion that, apparently, things haven't changed much in more than fifty years of medical practice.

Here are the symptoms in a few of the patients diagnosed by Doctor Kerr and colleagues with hyperventilation syndrome:

- Case 3: female, age 21—chief complaints: convulsive seizures, fatiguability, flushing of face and chest, headache, abdominal gas, carpopedal spasms, insomnia. Medical examination reveals nothing except slightly dilated pupils and hyperactive reflexes.
- Case 8: male, age 27—chief complaint: grand mal convulsions. Physical examination shows nothing other than Chvostek's sign (a puckering of the mouth when a region of the face is tapped lightly), a symptom of hyperventilation.
- Case 10: female, age 27—chief complaints: precordial chest pain, weakness, easy fatiguability, muscle twitches, dyspnea, nausea, right occipital headache with photophobia (light sensitivity). Physical examination shows nothing other than Chvostek's sign and hyperactive reflexes.

But a complete listing of all the different complaints and symptoms reported in the thirty-five cases they published includes:

Neurological:
- hyperactive reflexes
- headaches
- grand mal seizures
- vertigo (dizziness)
- paresthesia (tingling sensations in hands, feet, etc.)
- nervousness
- irritability

In the head and neck region:
- dyspnea (". . . can't catch my breath. I feel like I am choking.")
- inability to swallow (constricted throat or throat muscle stiffness)
- headaches
- Chvostek's sign
- migraine
- photophobia (light sensitivity)
- puckering sensation about the mouth
- flushing of face
- tinnitus (ringing in ears)

In the chest and abdominal region:
- abdominal gaseous distention
- chest pain
- hypertension
- precordial pain, with or without pain radiating to right or left arm, or to scapula
- tachycardia (rapid pulse)
- palpitations
- angina
- epigastric pain
- colitis
- diarrhea

In arms and legs:
- aching hands and feet
- Raynaud's (cold fingers and toes, with spasms)
- allergic dermatitis
- numbness, stiffness, and/or spasms in hands and/or feet
- tetany
- carpopedal spasms

General:
- easy fatiguability

If we look at these thirty-five cases, we find that there is one instance of each of the following medical conditions: rheumatic heart disease with mitral stenosis and insufficiency, thyroid nodule, splenomegaly, thyroid adenoma, skin lesions, hemorrhoids, and arteriosclerosis with a systolic murmur.

Eight symptoms in thirty-five cases! But in eight of these cases, physical examination revealed absolutely nothing. In twenty-four cases, the only finding was hyperactive reflexes with or without Chvostek's sign.[11]

It would seem that, except that they are very nervous, these patients give evidence of fewer dread illnesses than one might expect. In fact, it has been shown in a medical study that these symptoms do not lead to an early death. And yet these patients are not well.

Medicine's Confusion about Hyperventilation

One particular medical report, dating back to Civil War days, is an enlightening illustration of the reasons why it has been so difficult to establish the role of hyperventilation in health and disease.

At the time of the Civil War, a military field surgeon named J. M. DaCosta first described a number of complaints reported by soldiers. This symptom pattern came to bear his name—DaCosta's syndrome. It centered on an apparent loss of physical stamina and, consequently, an inability to carry out field duties. Subsequently, DaCosta's syndrome came to be known variously as neurocirculatory asthenia, anxiety neurosis, or effort syndrome.

A number of medical sources have attributed the following symptoms to those diagnostic terms: breathlessness, palpitations, chest pain, nervousness, fatigue, headache, dizziness, sighing, attacks or spells, apprehension, trembling and discomfort in crowded places.[12]

These bear a striking resemblance to symptoms of anxiety—in the extreme case, panic with agoraphobia. But if hyperventilation is a "hysterical" manifestation, as Dr. Thomas P. Lowry suggested,[13] then it is not a medical entity in the ordinary sense of the word. Therefore, all these medical symptoms could not possibly be caused by it. So what does cause them?

What has proved most confusing, in the end, is that while Doctor Kerr and colleagues noted only a very few medical symptoms, they listed the following "other" symptoms experienced by their patients with hyperventilation syndrome:

- palpitations
- tires easily
- breathlessness
- nervousness
- chest pain
- sighing
- dizziness
- faintness
- apprehension

- headaches
- paresthesia
- weakness
- trembling
- unsatisfactory breath
- insomnia
- unhappiness
- shakiness
- fatigued all the time
- sweating
- fear of death
- smothering
- syncope
- flushes
- yawning
- pain radiating to left arm
- vascular throbbing
- dry mouth

This is clearly not a conventional list of medical symptoms, but it is comprehensive, and—except for a few items—it could just as well be a list of stress-related, anxiety, and psychophysiological disorder symptoms.

Physicians are taught that breathlessness is a medical disorder with some psychological symptoms. But psychiatrists, also trained in medicine, hold that breathlessness is a psychological disorder with some psychophysiological medical symptoms. None of them now recognizes hyperventilation syndrome.

Numerous other such symptoms lists have appeared over the years, and there is little point in repeating them here. They are all pretty much the same.[14]

Hyperventilation syndrome, a breathing disorder, seems to play a major role in most of the so-called psychophysiological and stress-related disorders.

The average medical practitioner is mostly unaware of the role now ascribed to hyperventilation in common cardiovascular and circulatory disorders; arrhythmias; hypertension; migraine; musculoskeletal spasms and chronic muscle fatigue; neurological disorders, including idiopathic epilepsy; stress-related disorders, including headache; and emotional disorders such as panic attacks and agoraphobia and depression. Medicine is still largely uncertain about the role of hyperventilation in many patient's complaints, even though medical education teaches the physiological disturbances it causes.

What If I Am on Medication?

Some medications may mimic the hyperventilation challenge in that they may worsen breathing and also tend to induce some of the symptoms common in hyperventilation, such as lightheadedness, dizziness, a sense of unreality, alteration in consciousness, and various strange sensations—all also common in prolonged anxiety and panic disorder.

It is important, therefore, if you take prescription or other medications, that you determine their side effects as well as their main effects. It may surprise you to see how many of these can involve breathing.

Here is a small sample of some common medications taken by some of my clients that may affect their breathing. The *Physicians' Desk Reference*, commonly known as the *PDR*, tells us the following:

Benadryl (Parke-Davis)—an antihistamine: dryness of mouth, nose, and throat, dizziness, thickening of bronchial secretions, tightness of chest.

Bumex (Roche)—a diuretic: hyperventilation (in 0.1 percent of cases).

Buspar (Mead Johnson)—anxiolytic (antianxiety): hyperventilation, shortness of breath, chest congestion (between 1/100 and 1/1,000 cases).

Cardizem (Marion)—a calcium channel blocker: breathing difficulty, irregular or fast-pounding heartbeat, dizziness or lightheadedness.

Empirin with Codeine (Burroughs Wellcome)—analgesic, anti-inflammatory, antipyretic (fever reducing): depression of respiration, lightheadedness, dizziness, said to be among the "most frequently observed adverse reactions to codeine." Chronic use of large doses of aspirin may lead to *salicylism*, whose manifestations may include hyperpnea (increased respiration), and hyperventilation.

Primaxin (Merck Sharp & Dohme)—antibiotic: dizziness and psychic disturbance, chest discomfort, dyspnea, hyperventilation (all less than 0.02 percent).

Prozac (Dista)—antidepressant: nervousness, anxiety, insomnia, dizziness, anorexia.

Voltaren (Geigy)—anti-inflammatory, analgesic, antipyretic: dizziness, appetite change, asthma, eczema/dermatitis (rash), urticaria (itch), depression, insomnia, anxiety, irritability, blurred vision, scotoma, palpitation, tachycardia, impotence, dyspnea, hyperventilation, paresthesia (strange skin sensations), memory disturbances, excess perspiration (all less than 1 percent).

Xanax (Upjohn)—antianxiety: lightheadedness, nervousness, fatigue, confusion.[15]

I have not listed medications here where breathing-related disorders resulted from overdose. It is not my intent to scare you away from medication, but to alert you to the possibility of its breathing-related effects.

Valerie: Chronic Fatigue

Valerie is a forty-two-year-old married woman, successful in a public relations career. She is of average height and weight, and walks erect, in spite of her chronic fatigue. Her handshake is strong and her hands are warm.

She complained of chronic tiredness and fatigue, which she reported battling more or less successfully each day. But by evening, she reported feeling worn out. She has no history of thyroid problems or anemia that might account for her tiredness.

In addition, she reported having had Epstein-Barr (EB) symptoms some time in the past. I referred her to a medical colleague to retest thyroid function and see if she might, nevertheless, also be anemic. The tests came back negative, and we proceeded on the basis that it might be a recurrence of the EB virus.

Initially, she was chest breathing at a rate of 21 b/min with very low carbon dioxide (3.52 percent). This is moderate to severe hyperventilation. But by the end of the first training session, she had good, though brief, control of her breathing: Her breathing rate dropped to 4.5 b/min and her carbon dioxide rose to 4.52 percent—at the lower end of normal.

The physician to whom she was referred also gave her some nutritional advice and a prescription for multiple vitamins. She returned for breathing training, once per week for five weeks. Her breathing improved with each practice session and she reported feeling much improved, for the first time in over a year.

During the last session, before terminating treatment, she revealed that she was now practicing breathing regularly, twice per day, and on an ad-lib basis, when she felt tired or tense.

Hyperventilation is well known to cause arterial blood vessels throughout the body to constrict, causing impaired blood flow to the body and to the brain. In addition, it adversely affects the acid-base balance of the body, causing all sorts of metabolic repercussions. Medicine generally recognizes the symptoms of the hyperventilation syndrome (HVS), but it attributes them to anxiety, while psychiatry holds the very same set of symptoms to indicate subconscious conflict translated into psychophysiological disorders.

Consequently, if your breathing appears to fit that described here, if you have any of these symptoms, and if those symptoms could not be explained by your physician, and were blamed on your mind rather than your body, you may just for once have bought the right book.

Phobias

Some folks experience inexplicable and irrationally strong fear reactions when confronted with some of the most common things, situations, or even ideas. They will go to elaborate lengths to avoid them. When these avoidance reactions interfere significantly with their life, it is said that they suffer phobias.

Stanley: Fear of Bridges

"The problem, Doc, is that I've just got to get back and forth across the river because that's where my job is . . . in Long Island City. And it's getting more difficult each time. In fact, now, Doc, when I even think about going across that bridge I just know that I'm going to panic. I mean . . . my breathing gets completely out of control, my hands get cold and clammy and I sweat, and I'm incredibly anxious . . . even at the thought of it. I can feel my chest tighten when I just talk about it."

Stanley is describing the symptoms of a phobia that he's had for some years and that seems to be getting gradually worse—a bridge phobia.

"The weird part, Doc, is that I know that I'm not afraid of bridges. It's not like I think that the bridge is going to collapse as I cross it. I don't know what it is exactly. What do you think, Doc?"

"Well, Stanley, I propose that we begin to treat your phobia with breathing exercises that are meant to reduce your anxiety about crossing bridges."

"That sounds okay to me, Doc. But why is breathing going to get me across that bridge?"

"You've told me yourself, Stanley, that you are not afraid of bridges. And I believe you. Let me explain. When people have a phobia, it could be about an object like your bridge, or a snake, or a spider, or a situation like a social gathering, or speaking in public.

"They will readily identify the object or the situation. But in fact, it's not the object or the situation that's causing their anxiety. Because those things don't have an inherent power to do that. For instance, most persons are not afraid to cross bridges. Their phobia comes from the scary body sensations that the object or situation induces in them. In other words, you don't fear the bridge, you fear the body sensations that occur in connection with bridges. The word 'connection' means conditioning. You have developed a conditioned aversion to bridges."

"Yeah, Doc, but where does breathing come into the picture?"

"Well, Stanley, you've told me yourself that the first thing that happens in your body is that your breathing gets out of control. That starts the process of anxiety. If you can learn to keep your breathing from going out of control then you can learn to stop the sensations that you fear even before they start. That's why we begin with breathing training."

The most acclaimed recent developments in the treatment of stress-related and anxiety disorders have been in biofeedback and self-regulation. These advances rely principally on our increasing knowledge of how the nervous system works, and ways in which behavior becomes learned, or conditioned. It is generally believed that many of the answers to the whys of these disorders may be found here. Even cognitive behavior therapies that address thoughts and feelings take into account the natural and conditioned triggers of anxiety, anger, frustration, stress, and depression.

It may interest you to know, parenthetically, that the origin of the word "anxiety" is the ancient Greek word that means "to choke." Disrupted breathing has long been recognized to be related to emotions.

Michael: Fear of Dogs

Michael is a forty-one-year-old corporate attorney. He lives with his wife and two children in a suburban community. His medical and psychological history is mostly uneventful. Nevertheless, there was this one problem: He came to see me for treatment of a dog phobia to which he generally only admitted with considerable reluctance. Michael thought that his dog phobia was irrational and unbecoming, and he went to great lengths to avoid revealing it to anyone outside his family.

In cases like Michael's, treatment procedure commonly includes an assessment of the impact that the phobia exerts on the bodily sensations he experiences by means of *continuous capnography.*

The capnograph is a continuous, computer-generated tracing of the breathing pattern based on the concentration of carbon dioxide in end-tidal breath. It is obtained by slightly inserting a slender section of rubber tubing at the entrance of the right nostril and taping it to the upper lip. The tubing leads to a carbon dioxide gas analyzer (capnometer), which transmits information about breathing to the computer.

No effort was made to deal with the dog phobia in the first few sessions. Instead, Michael was taught deep diaphragmatic breathing (see chapter 4) as the first tool in conquering it. When he had reached a comfortable breathing rate of five breaths per minute with normal carbon dioxide concentration, he was instructed to close his eyes and to imagine that he was standing in front of his house and that he could see a woman walking a dog on a leash about a block away.

Figure 2 shows Michael's capnograph as he was given the instruction to imagine that scene. As Michael inhaled (far left), the tracing is at zero. As he exhaled, the tracing shows an increasing carbon dioxide concentration as it goes from zero to 5 percent. But note that the expiration part of the tracing is interrupted by a hyperventilatory sawtooth pattern that reflects his loss of control over his breathing as he began to imagine the object of his phobia.

Michael continued to practice breath control together with muscle relaxation exercises to counter his anxiety response to the dog. In several weeks he conquered his phobia, evidenced by the disappearance of the sawtooth pattern in his breathing when he imagined a scene including a dog.

Automatic reflex reactions to perceived threats in our surroundings can become habitual, and we may then covertly act as if they are always present by rehashing them in our mind. This message speaks to our modern world: both real and imagined dangers, and the process of determining the appropriate response, may be just as stressful because the same anxiety is evoked in either case.

Anxiety mimics the internal preparation for action. When action follows, the state dissipates. But when action is inhibited or the dreaded event does not happen, we nevertheless may maintain arousal. In those cases where there is preparation for action, but no need for that action, it takes longer to restore the body.

This is also why using breathing exercises to relax at home, or periodically in the office or other place of employment, is so impor-

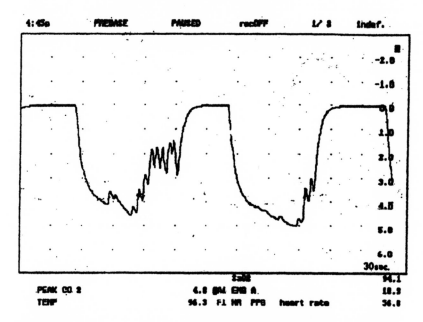

Figure 2 One-minute sample of breathing pattern showing loss of control during eyes-closed imagining of scene about the object of phobia.

tant. By reducing the action-oriented muscle tension, and blood levels of hormones and fuel, relaxation creates an internal environment that is in harmony with the external environment.

Action or anxiety can be conditioned to trivial environmental happenings. These then become our own special master switches and we become their slaves, as you saw above in the case of Michael. But through breathing control, you can learn to weaken the action of those same switches.

PART TWO

Taking Action to Feel Better

CHAPTER 4

The Five-Day Program
for Better Breathing
and Relaxation

Stress—Everybody Has It
but Nobody Knows What It Is

Ask anybody "Do you have stress?" I guarantee that the answer will be a resounding yes. Now ask, "What do you actually have when you have stress?" There will be a quick "Well . . ." followed by considerable hesitation, and the answer will be some time in coming. Finally, it will boil down to muscle tension, anxiety, and discomfort.

You could, of course, point out that this is exactly what people feel on a roller-coaster ride at the amusement park, to which they subject themselves voluntarily—even paying for the privilege—and which they report to be fun.

Therefore, it can be concluded that stress is a phenomenon that one experiences in a particular context. For example:

- You are sitting at the speaker's table. Your turn to address the audience is rapidly approaching. You are well rehearsed, yet you fear that you will not remember the speech you have prepared.

Your throat is drying up and you tense up as anxiety and apprehension are mounting to almost unbearable levels. Your hands grow cold and begin to sweat, and your breath is short and rapid—you can't focus on the group before you—everything is a blur. It is becoming increasingly clear to you that you are bound to stumble and make a complete fool of yourself. . . .

- You are buckling your safety belt. Although others are still stowing luggage in the overhead bins, the doors of the passenger cabin are closing and the flight attendants are preparing for departure. An overwhelming foreboding of doom is beginning to infiltrate every fiber of your body. Your throat clamps up and you can't catch your breath. You grasp the arm rests in an effort to hang onto something. You feel as though your skin is compressing your body. You are dizzy and faint. It is becoming increasingly clear to you that you simply have to escape from this situation because, if you do not crash on takeoff, you will surely die of a heart attack or stroke caused by the anxiety, or so the sensations in your chest seem to indicate. You feel that you are losing control. . . .

- You are sitting at home, staring into your coffee. You must go to the office. Inexplicably, of late, you feel apprehension, leading to terror, at the prospect of leaving your home. You know that as soon as you even begin to think of going outside, you begin to hyperventilate and to feel faint. The rapid pounding sensations in your chest suggest a heart attack. And you know that, at the very least, you will not be on the street long before you lose control and pass out. . . .

- You realize that the sudden worsening of your chronic colitis may be directly related to the fact that, although your work performance was said by your supervisor to be exemplary, you were once again passed up for promotion. Now you sit at your desk mulling over this injustice and feeling more and more depressed and anxious as you wonder whether this "oversight" may not portend a sudden announcement that, for the sake of economy, the office is undergoing a staff reduction. . . .

Whatever it may be, stress and anxiety are costly to the body's energy economy. That's because you are biologically designed to ward off all sorts of momentary dangers, but you are not prepared to do so on a continuous basis.

Mechanisms designed to cope with danger require resources, nutrients, vitamins and minerals, enzymes, and neurotransmitters, manufactured as needed or stored in the body, to be expended in relatively enormous quantities—sometimes far greater than the body can afford to sustain indefinitely. This expenditure results in a deficit which, in the long run, may be a major contribution to stress symptoms, anxiety, and depression.

Stress is usually reported to be accompanied by the following:

- chronic shortness of breath and sighing respiration
- chronic tiredness
- depression
- inability to concentrate
- impaired memory
- irritability
- anxiety
- various aches and pains
- aggravation of symptoms of medical disorders

Reducing stress requires that you manage your resources, conserving them where appropriate, replenishing them where loss is unavoidable. And that includes oxygen. The addition of deep diaphragmatic breathing, both in a daily routine and on an as-needed, preventive basis is one of the most effective means available to you to help protect and manage your body resources.

Periodically taking a few abdominal (diaphragmatic) breaths is the quickest, easiest, and most effective way of countering anxiety and assuring body and brain tissue oxygenation. It can be done anywhere, in such a way that no one needs to know you are doing it. And it costs nothing to do it. Integrating a few abdominal breaths, once or twice, into your daily routine may lead, down the road, to its becoming automatic.

A Word about Attitude

A thought can initiate or forestall action. Science has shown that if you think about moving your arm, there will be imperceptible contractions of the arm muscles involved. That would not appear to involve learning. If you imagine throwing a dart at a dartboard, and you imagine that it strikes the bull's-eye, that will actually help you to improve your skill, because the imperceptible movements associated with this covert practice improve actual performance.

There are thoughts, such as *I can do it*, that help, and there are weakening thoughts, such as *I can't do it. It won't work.* These thoughts function like covert practice, whose imperceptible effects affect performance. Keep that in mind.

Now let's enter into a contract.

AGREEMENT TO IMPROVE MY ATTITUDE
I, _____, on this, the _____ of
_____ _____ agree that I will take great care to avoid using phrases such as:
   "I can't."
   "You can't."
   "It won't work."
   "This is too hard to do."
   "I will never get better."
   "It will always be like this."
And if I catch myself making any of these statements, I will say to myself:
   "I can do it."
   "If I try, it will work. Maybe not right away, but with practice it will work. This is not too hard to do and it is good for me, too. I will get better."
   "It wasn't always like this and it will be better again."
And each time that I remember to do this, I will say to myself, "Good! I Remembered."
Signed: _____
                    [You]

Rapid Alert Relaxation (RAR™)

This exercise combines deep abdominal breathing with mental imagery. It was developed as part of the ARTSystem™ (Alert Relaxation Training System) for the Prudential Insurance Co., and I have used it in the treatment of breathing, stress-related, anxiety, and psychophysiological disorders, including the following conditions:

- tension and anxiety
- burnout syndrome
- chronic anxiety disorder
- panic disorder (and agoraphobia)
- simple phobias (social, public speaking, etc.)
- depression
- tension headache
- migraine
- hypertension
- hyperventilation
- Raynaud's disease
- TMJ/bruxism (jaw clenching and teeth grinding)
- asthma
- idiopathic seizures
- gastritis
- irritable bowel/colitis/ileitis
- hypoglycemia
- diabetes
- insomnia
- aerophagia (burping)
- hyperhydrosis (wet hands)

Breathing training is, of necessity, a part of the treatment program. A successful treatment program may need to combine medical management of the disorders by a competent physician and medication, with nutrition, where necessary, as well as counseling, cognitive or other behavior modification, biofeedback/self-regulation, and other muscle relaxation training.

A NOTE OF CAUTION: Deep abdominal/diaphragmatic breathing may initially be strenuous for the person who has been holding the diaphragm in partial contraction as part of the physical stress profile. Diaphragmatic cramps are not unheard of. Should they occur and be anything but mild, or should they persist, discontinue the exercise immediately. *If an exercise causes you to feel pain or discomfort, stop immediately.*

A SECOND NOTE OF CAUTION: Do not do any exercise if you have any physical condition that would contraindicate its safety or benefits, or for which you are not fit by virtue of a physical condition or injury. Among such conditions are:

- A condition involving muscle or other tissue or organ malformation or injury; for example, sprained or torn muscles, torticolis (a curvature of the spine), fractures, recent surgery, etc.
- Any condition in which there is metabolic acidosis, for which hyperventilation may be compensatory (diabetes, kidney disease, etc.). *If in doubt, consult a physician.*
- Low blood pressure, or any related condition, such as syncope (fainting). Deep abdominal breathing may cause a significant decrease in blood pressure. Do not do it if you suffer from these conditions.
- Insulin-dependent diabetes. If you have this condition, you should not do this, or any other deep relaxation exercise, without the express approval of your physician and his/her close monitoring of your insulin needs. In the long run, deep relaxation may be beneficial in the management of diabetes, but the sudden reduction in the blood level of the stress hormones has been demonstrated to reduce insulin dependence. Under certain circumstances, hyperventilation may be the body's protection against diabetic acidosis.

Muscle Exercises for Relaxation

If I were to teach you relaxation or breathing in my office, you would be sitting comfortably in a high-back chair listening to my instructions, or imagining yourself at the beach or in another relaxing setting of your choice. Sometimes the background might be music or ocean sounds.

But before reaching this stage you would have learned to do rapid muscle relaxation and sustained abdominal (diaphragmatic) breathing. This is a skill that may take several weekly training sessions to acquire.

I have tried to program the instructions that follow in such a way as to make it possible for you to develop the same level of skill. But you are at a slight disadvantage: instead of relaxing and following verbal instructions, you must read them first, remember them, and then follow them with eyes closed.

1. Sit comfortably in your favorite chair. Sit as far back in the chair as you can so that the back of the chair supports your back. Your back should be more or less straight, forming a right angle with your thighs. Your calves should also be at a right angle to your thighs. Feet should be flat on the floor, four to five inches apart.

   Open your jacket or vest. Loosen your collar or tie. Loosen any tight belt or garment restricting abdominal expansion.

   Place your hands in your lap and begin to let yourself slow down and relax. Let the weight in your upper body and torso drift down so that all your weight is supported by your buttocks and your thighs in contact with the chair.

   CAUTION: Always tense and relax muscles slowly. It does nothing to help you relax when you jerk or snap muscles. And it is very easy to hurt yourself unless you proceed very gently.

2. Extend your legs forward, keeping your heels on the ground. Point your toes forward until you feel the tension in your calves and ankles. Hold the tension to a count of five: "One . . . two . . . three . . . four . . . five."

   Then relax slowly and gently.

   Could you feel the tension? Good.

   Repeat this procedure.

3. Bring your legs back so that your feet are flat on the floor, about five inches apart. Now press your feet down onto the floor as hard as you can—don't tip your chair backward. Hold to a count of five.

   Then relax gently.

   Could you feel the tension in your calves? In your thighs? If you could, good.

   Now repeat the procedure.
4. Imagine that there is a string encircling your body around your abdomen (belly). Now push out your abdomen, slowly, as if you wished to break that string. Hold the tension to a count of five.

   Then relax slowly and gently.

   Could you feel the tension in your abdomen? In the small of your back? If you could, good. If not, try again a little later.

   This is a diaphragm contraction exercise. Contraction of your diaphragm pushed your abdomen out. That, parenthetically, is why we call diaphragmatic breathing abdominal or belly breathing. Since the diaphragm is also attached at the lower back, you may feel tension there also when contracting it. Did you?

   Now repeat this procedure.
5. Raise your arms forward to a horizontal position, parallel to the ground, and extend them forward keeping your hands limp, as if you were reaching for something in front of you. Now, with your body remaining in place, reach forward as far as you can, one arm at a time if necessary.

   Hold it for a count of five. Then relax gently and bring your arms slowly back to their original position.
6. Raise your arms forward to a horizontal position, parallel to the ground. Now bend your elbows to form a right angle. Contract your biceps muscles, as hard as you can, and hold to a count of five.

   Then relax gently.

   Could you feel the tension in your arms? Your shoulders? Repeat.

7. Gently raise your shoulders as high as you can, keeping your head in a straight line with your back. Hold to a count of five.

   Now relax gently.

   Could you feel the tension in your neck and shoulders?

   Repeat this procedure.

8. Close your eyes and squeeze your forehead by frowning. Purse your lips as if you wished to kiss someone. Do this as hard as you can. Hold to a count of five.

   Now relax gently.

   Repeat the procedure.

9. Start with your head upright in a straight line with your back, and tilt it to the left. Do not turn your head to the left, but tilt it. When you feel the tension in your right shoulder and arm, shake your right arm to release the tension.

   Hold it for just a moment.

   Now tilt your head a little more to the left. As the tension mounts in your right shoulder and arm, shake the right arm to release the tension.

   Hold it for just a moment.

   Now slowly bring your head back to the start position and hold it that way for a moment.

10. Start with your head upright in a straight line with your back, and tilt it to the right. Do not turn your head to the right, but tilt it. When you feel the tension in your left shoulder and arm, shake your left arm to release the tension.

    Hold it for just a moment.

    Now tilt your head a little more to the right. As the tension mounts in your left shoulder and arm, shake the left arm to release the tension.

    Hold it for just a moment.

    Now slowly bring your head back to the start position. How do you feel? Do you feel more relaxed and less tense overall?

The above exercise is a moderate muscle relaxation exercise, and varying versions of it are widely used to reduce muscle tension and anxiety. Some practitioners prefer to reverse the sequence, starting at the head and working toward the toes. If you prefer that sequence, by all means do it that way.

Abdominal (or Diaphragmatic) Breathing: A Five-Day Program

Here is an abdominal breathing training exercise that I often have used successfully to correct rapid, shallow chest breathing and to promote relaxation. It helps reduce muscle tension, pulse rate, and blood pressure, and promotes a general sense of alert well-being, relaxation, and comfort.

Since many of you who will try the following exercise have not done anything like it before, I have broken down the training procedures into several days, so that your muscles will have time to adjust and become toned for this task.

It is generally a good idea to do deep abdominal breathing exercises slowly at first, without straining the diaphragm. The emphasis is on comfort. You are not trying to add bulk to muscles, like a weight lifter. You are actually relearning a skill that you once had quite naturally, as an infant.

This is a different form of aerobics where you are trying to increase oxygenation of the body by increasing the efficiency of breathing. If you experience pain and discomfort, you are doing it wrong.

In preparation, you will have to read through all the instructions before beginning each exercise so that you can learn the steps and do them, when necessary, with your eyes closed.

Day 1

Seat yourself comfortably in your chair. Sit all the way back so that your back is supported by the back of the chair. Unbutton your collar. Loosen your tie, belt, or any other tight-fitting clothing. Place your hands on your knees and pause for a moment.

Place your left hand on your chest, just over your breastbone, and your right hand over your abdomen (over your belly button).

Look at your hands as you breathe. What is the left hand doing? What is the right hand doing? Are they moving together?

Your left hand, over your chest, should not be moving as you breathe in and out. And your right hand, over your abdomen, should be moving *out* as you *inhale*, and *in* as you *exhale*.

Check and make sure that you are doing this:

Breathe IN > Belly OUT
Breathe OUT > Belly IN

Repeat three times, then stop. Do you feel dizzy? If not, good.

If you feel dizzy, you are overbreathing (hyperventilating). This means that you are putting too much effort into it too early in the game. You are moving too much air out of your lungs too quickly. Make the motions a little more subtle; not so far out on inhale and not so far in on exhale. You will soon improve if you do not over-practice.

But if you feel dizzy, stop and rest a little while until the dizziness passes. The initial dizziness should disappear after a few practice sessions. Rarely, it may not stop.

If you do not stop feeling dizzy after a few practice sessions, stop trying the exercise because it may mean that your breathing is compensating for metabolic acidosis, and it may be wisely resisting your efforts to change it.

Note: If your left hand is moving predominantly, or if both hands are rising and falling at the same time, you are breathing with your chest. Or is the movement of your hands shallow and slow, or shallow and rapid? Make a note to yourself.

Close your mouth: breathe through your nose only. (Yes, in and out through the nose.)

I emphasize: Do not breathe through your mouth. It tends to promote overbreathing (hyperventilation). Breathing through the nose is healthier for you. The nose prepares the air for you: it cleans, warms, and moisturizes it.

Breathing through the nose will also keep the nasal passages warm. Among other things, this will reduce your likelihood of catching a cold. Cold viruses are deposited in the nose. They begin to multiply when the temperature in the nasal mucous tissue reaches a certain narrow low temperature range. Breathing through the nose keeps it warm and moist.

Look at your hands: As you inhale, hold your chest and don't let it rise. Let the hand on your abdomen rise as the air "fills your abdomen."

In fact, the air is not filling your abdomen. The air is filling your lungs, and when you can't raise your chest your lungs will fill by contraction of the diaphragm. This pushes out your abdomen, giving the impression that it is filling with air.

If you are uncertain about what to do, try the following procedure: Place a book on your lap (spine up, so that it won't slide off). Now, without coordinating it with your breath at all, push the book out as far as you can with your abdomen.

When you inhale, and you are filling up with air, your abdomen should move out about as far as it did when you pushed the book. If you find that the book did not move out much, don't worry. If you are tense and tight, that is to be expected. You will improve with practice.

On exhale: slowly—but never so slowly that it creates discomfort—pull your abdomen back as far as it will go, but do not let it raise your chest.

Good. Now, don't stop. Don't pause; repeat the inhale and exhale procedure once more.

Rest for a moment.

You will find, after a few days of practicing just three to four minutes per day—don't do more, now—that your inhale and exhale will be of approximately the same duration. There should be no pause in breathing—not before or after inhale or exhale—just one smooth motion. Your breathing rate may range between three and seven breaths per minute. If you continue to do this exercise, you may soon notice how good it feels.

The emphasis is on comfort. You are doing a difficult exercise: Your diaphragm is a very large muscle and you are contracting it, then you are pushing it back in place with your abdominal muscles. This is heavy work. It is strenuous, and you will benefit from the exercise only if you do it in moderation and do not permit the muscles to get tired. Exercising tired muscles does not improve them.

Now, once again: inhale . . . fill up. And exhale . . . pull all the way back. Repeat this procedure three times, then stop. That's all for today.

If you do more than this, it may be counterproductive and may result in diaphragmatic cramps. You may be a little dizzy. That should pass. Don't stand up suddenly if you feel dizzy.

You may have a slight tendency to overbreathe (hyperventilate) at first. Many of my clients do. It will pass and, with practice, it will disappear. So take my advice: Wait until tomorrow to continue.

Day 2

Prepare yourself for the exercise in the same way as you did yesterday. Sit back in your chair. Place your hands on your knees for a moment. Let yourself relax. Close your mouth.

Place your hands on your chest and abdomen as you did yesterday. Once you get the knack, you can do it without your hands. Now, looking at your hands, inhale, holding down your chest and letting your abdomen "fill up." Then, exhale slowly, and pull your abdomen all the way back.

Repeat this procedure three more times.

That's enough for today.

Did you find it to be any easier? Did your abdomen move farther out when you inhaled? Did the hand on your chest remain more or less motionless? Can you pull your abdomen a little farther in?

Notice that I recommend only very short exercise sessions the first few days. Your diaphragm and abdominal muscles need time to tone up.

Most persons who look to self-help may be at least a little compulsive and will overdo everything, including breathing exercise. Restrain yourself, please. You'll see, it will come along much faster that way. You will not be fighting against sore muscles.

Day 3

Let's see you do the exercise without your hands now. Prepare yourself in your chair as you did yesterday.

Try it. Does your chest remain more still as you inhale, and is your abdomen moving outward? If it is, good. If not, go back to using your hands.

But if you can, then proceed breathing in and out four times in a row—close your eyes. Good!

If you still need to use your hands, then proceed, eyes closed, and imagine what your hands are doing. Good.

That's it for today.

Day 4

Can you do abdominal breathing without your hands now? If you can, good. Then you may do the following exercise that way. Otherwise, keep your left hand on your chest and your right hand on your abdomen until you can do the exercise without the use of your hands.

You are, once again, seated comfortably back in your chair, with your hands resting on your thighs. After reading this, you will close your eyes and imagine that you are at the beach. It is midmorning, the sun is shining and warm, but not hot. Feel the warmth of the sun on your head . . . on your shoulders . . . on your arms. The sky is clear and you are standing on the beach and looking at the ocean. The ocean is calm.

Do you have this scene in your mind? Can you picture it? When you set the beach scene, be sure to set a scene with which you are familiar, a place where you have, perhaps, vacationed.

You may close your eyes once more, after adding the following to the beach scene:

As you look at the ocean, in your mind's eye, begin abdominal breathing. As you inhale, get a sense that you are breathing in ocean air, and get a sense that you can fill up your abdomen with air, saying to yourself:

"I feel awake, alert, and refreshed."

And as you breathe out, feel the tension in your body flow out with your breath, as you say to yourself:

"I feel relaxed, warm, and comfortable."

Do this for four breaths, then stop. After a few minutes of rest, repeat the procedure. That's all for today.

Day 5

Repeat the procedure, as you did yesterday, adding the following, eyes closed:

"As I am standing on the beach, and looking at the ocean, in my imagination, the sun is shining and warm, but not hot. I can feel the warmth of the sun on my shoulders, my head, and my arms. The sky is clear and the ocean is calm."

As you breathe in:

"I can see the surf rolling up on the beach toward my feet. And as I breathe out, I can see the surf rolling out again."

Continue for four consecutive breaths.

Can you picture this? If you can, good. Try it again for three consecutive breaths. And now, with the action of the surf rolling in when you inhale, say to yourself:

"I feel awake, alert, refreshed."

And with the surf rolling out, as you exhale, say:

"I feel relaxed, warm, and comfortable."

Try it. If you don't get it right away, don't be discouraged. It improves with very little practice.

Try four consecutive breaths, coordinating your inhale with the surf rolling up on the beach, and your saying to yourself:

"I feel awake, alert, and refreshed."

And, as the surf rolls out, as you exhale, say:

"I feel relaxed, warm, and comfortable."

I would recommend the following to you, if you wish to learn this exercise: Do it once in the morning and once in the afternoon or evening—not more for the first week or two. And definitely do not do more than four to five breaths, or rounds, each time.

If you do not strain your muscles, you may be amazed at how quickly you will become proficient at this type of breathing exercise.

After about three weeks, I usually recommend that you do the exercise in rounds of three: four or five breathing cycles and a few moments' rest, followed by a second round of four or five breathing cycles, followed by a moment's rest, and finally, a third round of four or five breaths.

Always start the first round easy—not too far out on inhale, not too far in on exhale. Then inhale a little more with each progressive round. You may or may not wish to precede a breathing exercise session with the active relaxation exercises. That is up to you.

These are the initial daily breathing exercises that have helped many of my clients to overcome tension, anxiety, and the other psychophysiological and stress-related disorders listed previously. When you have mastered these exercises, you may progress to using them in specific situations. Remember:

- Wherever you are sitting, adjust your posture as you would for the relaxation exercise, with your back against the back of the chair, your feet flat before you.
- If you can, loosen your clothing.
- Close your eyes, concentrate on abdominal breathing, and focus your attention on your nostrils. As you inhale, feel the cool, fresh air rushing into your nostrils. Experience that freshness. "Fill up" and say to yourself:

  "I feel awake, alert, and refreshed."

  As you exhale, you may not feel the air exiting your nostrils (it is at body temperature). Feel the tension and anxiety in your body flowing out with your breath and say to yourself:

  "I feel relaxed, warm, and comfortable."

In the next chapters I will show you how these breathing exercises may be integrated into a treatment program aimed at reducing your symptoms.

CHAPTER 5

Nutrition and Breathing

It's Hard to Breathe
When You Don't Feel Good

I once remarked to a client on our third session that he'd likely feel better if he practiced the breathing exercises regularly at home. He assured me that he was trying, but he added that "it's hard to breathe when you don't feel good."

Jack was fiftyish and a successful stockbroker in a major East Coast city. He was the recently divorced father of two college-age children. There was absolutely nothing unusual in his background or medical history.

Jack had come to me by way of a referral from his primary care physician, bringing with him a veritable cornucopia of diffuse complaints that fit no discernible pattern. But mostly he had headaches, and he had episodes of severe weakness. Anemias, Epstein-Barr, mononucleosis, and Lyme disease had all been pretty much ruled out, as were a host of other usual suspects.

His physician thought that Jack might be depressed and, since he was familiar with my work, he thought that breathing training might help Jack somehow. Jack was, indeed, moderately depressed, but this was principally due to his failure to find someone who would help him to get rid of his afflictions.

Jack's breathing was shallow, though not particularly rapid, and

77

on examination, his carbon dioxide concentration was found to be only slightly below normal. This sort of profile often suggests allergy. But I had no way of knowing, so I referred him to a physician colleague who was very savvy.

Jack, it turned out, had multiple food and other allergies. He was given nutritional counseling by that physician, and after some time, reported feeling well enough to engage in serious breathing training.

This case drives home the fact that ailments often exist in a context. It is easy to become so reliant on a treatment strategy that the horizon shrinks: it has been said that if all you have is a hammer, you may tend to treat everything as though it were a nail. And so, in Jack's case, I was reminded of the close relationship between nutrition and well-being as it relates to therapeutic breathing training.

Few today recall that the modern study of epilepsy really began when it was reported in 1901 by the illustrious neurologist Sir William R. Gowers, and again in 1924 by Dr. Joshua Rosett, that hyperventilation triggers seizures. Yet one of the earliest successful treatments for that disorder was the high-protein ketogenic diet, long forgotten as a treatment for seizures, but now resurrected for its ability to cause weight loss.

Nutrition plays an important general role in health and well-being, and there are many good books written on this topic. But its concern to you is that dietary factors have also been implicated in stress and anxiety disorders, most of which show disordered breathing.

Just as it is becoming increasingly apparent that such disorders affect breathing, so is it also increasingly evident that nutrition plays a key role in this interaction. I see this often in my clients. For instance, three of the more common foods I have found to be frequently responsible for allergic reactions involving breathing are milk, wheat, and corn. These are also at the top of the lists of foods to which most allergy sufferers respond positively.

Since the 1930s, medical journals have reported that there is strong evidence linking foods to anxiety, depression, migraine, and even childhood hyperactivity and autism.[1] These findings have generally been neglected by conventional medical practitioners. Yet these studies employ research techniques just like those used in modern medical research studies and are just as valid today as they were then.

This chapter will tell you a little about how some nutrient substances found in common foods may play either a positive or an adverse role in psychophysiological, stress-related, and breathing disorders.

This chapter is intended to inform you about what we know about the effect of certain foods on breathing-related disorders. I do not recommend that you consume or stop consuming any food substance without consulting a trained medical specialist. In addition to physicians, one might also consult a licensed nutritionist for guidance in these areas.

Foods That Can Impair Your Blood Circulation

There are substances found in common foods that may promote conditions in your body that adversely affect breathing and favor stress disorders. They are numerous. But the amino acid tyramine is among the better known.

Researchers at the National Heart Institute in Bethesda, Maryland, have also long known that common foods contain varying amounts of substances, especially some amino acids that are the very building blocks of the crucial nervous system and brain chemical messengers called *neurotransmitters*, such as acetylcholine, norepinephrine, serotonin, and dopamine, among others. These act as switches in the body, turning things on or off.

It would be helpful to you to be aware of foods that contain or promote the body's release of these various substances if you have a stress disorder, or suffer from elevated blood pressure, migraine, asthma, allergies, or any other condition on which they have been demonstrated to have a detrimental effect. All of these conditions, and many more, involve breathing.

Tyramine is an amino acid which, by its action in the body, partly or completely mimics the effects of the activating sympathetic branch of your autonomic nervous system, resulting in varying degrees of fight-or-flight arousal.

The building blocks of tyramine are present in varying amounts in most foods and are converted to tyramine as that food "ages" by the action of bacteria. Even refrigerated foods have increased tyramine levels, though that increase is slower than in food left out.

Leftovers in your refrigerator have a higher content of tyramine than the foods did when they were fresh and first prepared. This fact could be important to you if you suffer from high blood pressure and migraine, both of which can be triggered by tyramine.

When released into the bloodstream, tyramine constricts blood vessels, which in turn may increase blood pressure. It also accelerates breathing. But it is usually rapidly broken down by an enzyme, monoamine oxidase (MAO), limiting its effects.

However, the deactivation of MAO by MAO inhibitors such as the MAOI antidepressants Nardil and Marplan may prevent the catabolic breakdown of tyramine, resulting in an increase in blood pressure and leading to a dangerous elevation in blood pressure called a *hypertensive crisis*, and even possibly stroke. Alternatively, the blood pressure may fall precipitously instead of rising.

If you have suffered depression and have been prescribed MAO-type antidepressants, you may be well aware of the potential danger of hypertension and will have been cautioned about foods containing even the slightest quantities of tyramine. Tricyclic antidepressants, by the way, do not have this particular effect on MAO or on blood pressure. But those of you who have hypertension, were you told about tyramine by your doctor?

Yet it was reported in a medical journal that some persons may be naturally deficient in monoamine oxidase. Thus, it is advisable for you to be aware that there are foods that contain substances not inherently harmful to the ordinary person but whose effects may be of concern to you. I would remind you of the validity of the ancient Roman admonition, "One man's food is another's fierce poison."

While this need perhaps be of only minimal concern to most persons, it is a note of caution for others who may suffer from stress-related, anxiety, and psychophysiological disorders because tyramine quickens the pulse rate, raises blood pressure, and causes rapid breathing.

Some foods have a higher tyramine content than others. The *Mayo Clinic Diet Manual* informs us that the level of tyramine and other amines (proteins containing nitrogen) in food may be expected to show considerable variation due to the method of preparation, processing, and storage (both refrigerated and unrefrigerated).[2] The *Manual*, as well as other sources, suggest the following:

Beverages
Avoid: limit coffee, tea, and carbonated beverages to three cups per day.
Allowed: decaffeinated coffee, cereal beverages, and artificially flavored fruit drinks.

Meat and Cheese
Avoid: aged and processed cheese, pickled herring, dried herring, liver, peanuts and peanut butter, aged meats (including dry sausage, hard salami, pepperoni, and summer sausage), and any meats prepared with meat tenderizer or with soy sauce.
Allowed: cottage cheese, soft or semidry sausage, and cured meat.

Fat
Avoid: sour cream and avocados.
Allowed: cream cheese.

Milk
Avoid: chocolate milk and yogurt.
Allowed: all others.

Starch
Avoid: fava beans.
Allowed: all beans, including broad beans other than fava beans, and all other starches.

Vegetables
Avoid: sauerkraut, pickles, etc.
Allowed: all others.

Fruit
Avoid: canned figs, raisins, and raspberries.
Allowed: all others.
Soup
Avoid: commercial canned soup and any soup made with soup cubes or meat extracts.
Allowed: all others.
Desserts
Avoid: any made with chocolate.
Allowed: all others.
Sweets
Avoid: any containing chocolate.
Allowed: all others.
Miscellaneous
Avoid: meat tenderizer, meat or yeast extracts, brewer's yeast, soy sauce, chocolate, beer and wine and other alcoholic beverages.
Allowed: all others, including baker's yeast as a leavening agent in bakery products.

You might bear in mind that these recommendations, as well as those to follow, were compiled by various dietetic study groups because these foods are shown to increase blood pressure and therefore may be harmful to persons with borderline elevated blood pressure or hypertension, cardiovascular, circulatory, or vascular problems.

Missing from the above list is the caution to avoid smoked or cured meats (e.g., bacon, lox, and corned beef) and pickled vegetables. You should also be aware of the fact that the riper a given fruit, the greater the content of tyramine.

I have always found it amazing that despite the evidence (many hospitals distribute the list to heart patients), dietary recommendations by the average medical practitioner to persons with hypertension seldom mention anything other than low sodium. It is well known that the amino acid tyramine, which builds up in foods, may in some persons be so slowly converted by monoamine oxidase to its nontoxic form (parahydroxyphenylacetic acid) that its effects on blood pressure may pose a serious health hazard. Tyramine quickens breathing.

Here is another list compiled from such diverse sources as the *Archives of Biochemistry and Biophysics* and the *Mayo Clinic Diet Manual:*

Avoid: alcoholic beverages (including wine, beer, and ale), homemade yeast breads, crackers containing cheese, sour cream, bananas, red plums, avocados, figs, raisins, aged game, liver, canned meats, yeast extracts, commercial meat extracts, stored beef liver, chicken livers, salami, sausage, aged cheese (including blue, Boursault, brick, Brie, Camembert, cheddar, Colby, Emmentaler, Gouda, mozzarella, Parmesan, provolone, Romano, Roquefort, and Stilton), salted dried fish (herring, cod), pickled herring, Italian broad beans, green bean pods, eggplant, yeast concentrates or products made with them, marmite, soup cubes, commercial gravies, anything with soy sauce, and any protein that has not been stored properly or has some degree of spoilage (i.e., all but those that have been freshly prepared).

There is much overlap of these lists, some items appearing in one and not the other.

N. P. Sen reports the tyramine content of various standard foods in an article in the *Journal of Food Science*. Orange juice has relatively little tyramine, while the whole fruit is not allowed in one other list given above. Cheese is relatively high in tyramine, but content varies with the type and the sample taken from each type. Yeast and meat extracts are also quite high in tyramine, and so is salted dried herring. This particular list does not mention pickled herring, nor figs or plums, for instance.[3]

Because of the importance of this food list in migraine, hypertension, and other disorders, I am proposing that you consider tracking what you eat on the "What You Can Do" food list at the end of this chapter. It will give you a good idea of what suspect foods you consume, and how frequently you consume them. This may prove very helpful in determining their possible role in your symptoms.

Foods Can Give You Migraine

In addition to foods high in tyrosine, a tyramine building block (including bananas, plums, avocados, and eggplant), there are other foods, such as milk and turkey, that are rich in another amino acid, tryptophan. Tryptophan is a building block of one of the body's important neurotransmitter switches, serotonin, which features prominently in mood and chronic pain disorders.

Tyramine and tryptophan are among the body building blocks which have been linked to migraine, seizure disorders, and other neurological manifestations of allergic reactions. These reactions have been well documented, although medical research into this aspect of clinical practice is limited to the role of allergy to foodstuffs in childhood hyperactivity hyperkinetic syndrome, now called attention deficit hyperactivity disorder (ADHD).

There have been numerous published reports on food allergy in migraine; one of the best can be found in the *Lancet*, detailing the tyramine-rich foods known to contribute to migraine.[4]

I have combined the *Lancet* list with that of H. H. Davison, reported in the *Quarterly Review of Allergy and Applied Immunology*, and with others.[5] The items are listed below:

- milk, sour cream, yogurt
- wheat
- chocolate
- aged or processed cheese
- corn (and Karo syrup)
- alcohol (wine, beer, etc.)
- red meat (beef, etc.), pork (pork products)
- food containing monosodium glutamate (MSG)
- licorice
- eggs
- bouillon, soup cubes, soy sauce
- nuts (especially peanuts and peanut butter)
- pickled or marinated herring
- seafood, shellfish

- citrus fruit (oranges, grapefruit)
- cola drinks
- bananas
- tomatoes, cabbage, spinach, avocados
- canned soup
- chicken liver, beef liver
- processed foods and smoked or cured meats
- plums, prunes, canned figs
- raisins
- broad beans, lima beans
- coffee, tea, cocoa

These are among the better-known sources, though you may be sensitive to other foods. In a survey of research on food allergy and migraine, a recent *New York Times* article reported finding that "75% of migraine patients may be allergic to 5 or more foods . . . some to 20 or more foods."

If you are a parent, you are probably aware of the role of junk foods and stimulants such as caffeine found in soft drinks, preservatives, and coloring and additives, in migraine. I am sure that you've read about this in many magazines that report on health issues. But I would like to direct your attention to an article by Dr. J. Egger and colleagues, published in the *Journal of Pediatrics* and titled "Oligoantigenic Diet Treatment of Children with Epilepsy and Migraine." (Oligoantigenic means low in antigens, substances to which your immune system responds with the production of antibodies.) The foods mentioned most frequently were:

- cow milk
- cow cheese
- pork
- chocolate
- citrus fruit
- wheat
- corn
- grapes

- food additives
- tea
- hen eggs
- beef
- tomatoes
- cane sugar[6]

You might consider these items if you decide to consult a physician or nutritionist with a view to reducing them in your diet or in your child's diet. Remember, I recommend against going cold turkey on foods. Elimination diets should be supervised by a qualified professional. Sudden elimination of foods that trigger symptoms may actually aggravate the condition.

I have treated many migraine sufferers and virtually all had some form of breathing disorder, usually including hyperventilation. There is little doubt in my mind that sensitivity to some foods contributes to disordered breathing in a number of different ways.

Hyperventilation is a known trigger of epileptic seizures, and I can vouch for the role of both nutritional factors and breathing disturbances in that neurological disorder. For persons with seizures, migraine and, in some cases, asthma, my preferred "don't touch it" food list ranks:

- milk
- processed or aged cheese
- wheat
- chocolate
- pickled herring or pickled vegetables
- smoked or cured meats or fish
- corn
- bananas, plums, canned figs
- beef
- pork, turkey
- soy sauce
- nuts

- licorice
- broad beans
- eggplant, tomatoes, spinach
- citrus pulp, raspberries
- anything containing these foods

Naturally, bananas, for instance, do not cause headaches in everyone, but people who are sensitive to tyramine might be cautious.

Additionally, a list of inhalants suspected of triggering these disorders, especially asthma, includes:

- dog and cat dander or hair, bird feathers
- dust
- mold
- pollen
- tobacco
- common household cooking gas (leakage through pilot ignition flame)
- believe it or not, tiny pieces of the outer shell (exoskeleton) that fall off cockroaches as they crawl about in your home

These food substances and inhalants do not invariably trigger episodes of a neurological or respiratory disorder. Rather, they have been implicated often enough in these disorders to be taken seriously. There is still considerable controversy about which substances act and by what mechanism they act to promote these disorders.

My preferred explanation follows *catastrophe theory*, which attempts to explain when a constant relationship is observed to cause an unpredictable change. For instance, a constant pressure applied when bending a stick will result in a predictable bowing of the stick, up to a point. Beyond that point, it breaks. This would not be predicted from the initial changes in the stick due to bending. No matter how much information you have about bending sticks, you cannot predict exactly at what point they will break.

By the same token, a gradual increase in the blood level of action hormones or their mimics from recently consumed food, or increased histamine from an inhaled allergen, may not produce a *gradual* increase in symptoms. There may be a very gradual and imperceptible change taking place in the body, accompanied by an increase in breathing. Then beyond a certain point, symptoms emerge with vigor.

There is even evidence to suggest that this is what happens in seizure disorder. The effect of allergic stressors accumulates until the seizure threshold is surpassed. The action hormone mimics consumed in foods add to stress-related, naturally released action hormones, and breathing quickens. You begin to hyperventilate, and that may well be the factor that tips the balance.

Minerals and Breathing

My digression into foods is to make you aware of how nutrition can affect how you breathe. Thus, the mention of the following items is sketchy and intended to get you acquainted with what's what. It is up to you to follow up.

Proper levels of minerals in the body are essential to proper functioning. There are many forms of mineral deficiency that both impede health and are manifest in breathing disorders.

Iron

Oxygenated blood flows from the lungs, through the left heart, to the body tissues, where it delivers the oxygen and picks up carbon dioxide. It then returns to the lungs via the right heart, and the cycle repeats if all goes well. For the most part, oxygen is carried in the hemoglobin in red blood cells. The quantity of red blood cells in the blood is regulated by iron availability.

If there is an insufficiency of dietary iron available for the formation of red cells, anemia may follow rapidly. This is a condition characterized by pallor, weakness, loss of appetite, and a number of other symptoms including an increase in breathing rate, which frequently leads to hyperventilation.

Zinc

This trace mineral is involved in the body's storage of histamine and is an essential component in a wide range of enzymes, including RNA and DNA enzymes, and carbonic anhydrase, which is crucial to respiration.

Carbon dioxide in blood is converted through the action of carbonic anhydrase to bicarbonate and hydrogen ions exhaled by the lungs and expelled by the kidneys. This is part of the carbon dioxide elimination system and part of the process for maintaining the body's acid-base balance. Zinc is usually not toxic, and excess body zinc is virtually unknown.

Magnesium

This trace mineral is the fourth most abundant metal in the human body. It is essential to the proper function of the nervous system as well as the cardiovascular, vascular, and circulatory systems. It has been said to be the "mimic/antagonist" of calcium, which is the natural way that the body prevents excess calcium in tissues. While calcium is necessary to proper bone structure, its excess is detrimental to red blood cells, which it makes rigid, and to muscle, heart, and nerve cells, which become overactive.

In an article abstracted in the *Journal of the American College of Nutrition*, I reported that our epileptic clients who hyperventilated and did not respond well to anticonvulsant medication were deficient in tissue levels of magnesium even if blood serum levels were normal.[7]

Calcium

This mineral is found in all parts of the body, but 99 percent of it is found in your bones. It is essential to blood clotting and the ability of nerves and muscles to respond to stimulation. Calcium deficiency is far from rare: it is involved in rickets and osteoporosis.

Calcium is rapidly lost from the body by inactivity, especially bed rest. It has been strongly implicated in emotional and psychophysiological disorders; the treatment of depression, for instance, has been shown to increase calcium retention.

Potassium

This is the third major mineral in the body, next to calcium and phosphorus. Together with sodium, potassium regulates the electrical balance of cell membranes. It is therefore critical in the function of the lungs, the heart, blood vessels, and nerve fibers. Potassium deficiency, like magnesium deficiency, can be observed in changes in the electrical activity of the heart and in the reduced motility of the digestive tract, especially the stomach. It is a leading cause of chronic indigestion. Potassium helps to maintain the body's acid-base and fluid balance, which also directly affect breathing.

Other minerals, such as sodium, copper, and manganese, are also important, and I urge you to acquaint yourself with their role in your health. Any standard source, such as C. C. Pfeiffer's *Zinc and Other Micronutrients*,[8] may be helpful.

Vitamins and Breathing

There is much controversy about the role of vitamins in health and illness, and it usually centers on whether adequate levels can be obtained in the ordinary American diet. For example, the recommended daily allowance (RDA) for vitamin C is forty-five milligrams per day. But actually, this is only the minimum average daily quantity that will prevent scurvy. This says nothing about enhancing health. In fact, your doctor may prescribe greater daily doses just to control cystitis (urethral infection)—over one thousand milligrams per day.

Vitamin C is an essential vitamin. (All vitamins are "essential," because the body cannot make them. Their name is derived from "vital amine.") Among other things, vitamin C helps prevent anemia, and functions as a *free radical scavenger*, mopping up and preventing tissue damage due to dangerous concentrations in the blood of a variant form of oxygen called a *superoxygen free radical*.

One of the vitamins whose critical function in stress and psycho-physiological disorders is just beginning to become clear is vitamin B_6. Vitamin B_6 (pyridoxine) deficiency has been linked to neurological, breathing, and psychophysiological disorders, especially those in which hyperventilation has been implicated.

There have been reports of the role of vitamin B_6 deficiency in panic disorder and agoraphobia, a hyperventilation-related phenomenon. In one study, nutritional control, monitored by a functional vitamin/enzyme testing procedure, resulted in dramatic improvement in these "psychological" disorders. The deficiencies noted were in B_1, B_3, B_{12}, folic acid, and B_6.

This study also suggested that B_6 deficiency was due, in one case, to inadequate breakdown and absorption of that vitamin by the body. You may wish to keep in mind that the administration of pre-formed pyridoxal-5-phosphate (P-5-P), a metabolite of B_6, resolved the problem. P-5-P can be purchased in most health food stores. But supplementation of B_6 must be considered only with the advice of a physician, because an overdose can result in permanent adverse effects, including nerve damage.

Although vitamin B_6 is quickly lost when you are stressed, please don't self-prescribe.

Your body functions best when it is provided with certain essential nutrients—minerals and vitamins—and when you reduce the consumption of those that your body does not seem to agree with. That disagreement can be the cause of some of your symptoms. When it is coupled with an inherited or acquired predisposition, this constant food-related stress can also help to deplete the body more rapidly of its stores of nutrients, in some cases causing a critically low level of these constituents.

What You Can Do

Self-check to see if any of the foods you commonly consume are on the "suspect" food lists.

Instructions: Make a mark before the vertical line if you have consumed that food the first week, and after the vertical line if you've consumed it the following week.

Circle the day on which you either experienced the symptom(s) or, if chronic, it (they) worsened.

Table 1

	Sun	Mon	Tue	Wed	Thu	Fri	Sat
Milk, ice cream							
Wheat							
Chocolate							
Sugar							
Cheese (aged or processed)							
Spinach							
Corn (or products with Karo syrup)							
Citrus fruit							
Coffee (and/or tea)							
Alcohol							
Bananas							
Red meat							
Yeast/bouillon							
Sausage							
MSG							
Licorice							
Eggs							
Pork/pork products							
Nuts/peanut butter							
Pickled herring							
Seafood							
Cabbage							
Tomatoes							
Eggplant							
Chicken liver							
Processed foods							
Turkey							
Plums							
Salad bar salad							
Fried foods							
Cola							
Other							

CHAPTER 6

Breathing Applications in Common Complaints

Joan: Bad Body Vibes

Joan is a twenty-seven-year-old woman who sought help for her agoraphobia. While she was working at overcoming her problem through conventional psychotherapy she continued to manifest very subtle hyperventilation. She had experienced her first panic attack in a New York City subway following her attempt to run after a train and catch it because she was late for an appointment.

When it first happened, she thought that she was having a heart attack, and only later did she realize that her experience was anxiety. This spontaneous insight did not help her to cope with it. Subsequently, she began to fear having these attacks and avoided places such as trains, buses, automobiles, and elevators where she thought they might occur. She now also began to fear being away from a safe place, and she felt anxious whenever she left home.

The treatment strategy for Joan was broad-based and typical of the therapy for panic disorder patients who also have agoraphobia. Only a limited number of such patients respond to either conventional psychotherapy or to purely behavioral treatments. Therefore, in addition to cognitive therapy and behavioral therapy, she was given breathing retraining, which she learned in a few sessions.

Joan, like all agoraphobia sufferers, experiences fear of fear. In reality, it is fear of the strong aversive body sensations—"bad body vibes," she calls them—that the object(s) of her phobia or the situations in which they arise will cause her to experience. These include trembling, a frightening fear that she will choke, chest symptoms, and sweating. Her body will tense up as she awaits the next dreaded phase of the attack.

Such thoughts as these will run through her mind:

- *This time, that's it!*
- *I'll lose control.*
- *I can't stand this anxiety.*
- *I'll have an attack and I won't be able to deal with it.*
- *I'll be stranded, I'll faint or fall and make a fool of myself.*
- *This will never go away.*

Joan was taught to recognize how these thoughts resulted from her body vibes and, in turn, then aggravated them. As she became adept at diaphragmatic breathing, she discovered that she could actually inhibit these sensations.

There are many other instances when breathing may be used to counter anxiety and produce calm in the face of a phobic object or situation. For instance, you will recall our symposium speaker from chapter 4.

As he listens to his introduction to the participants, his eyes are closed momentarily. He is doing abdominal breathing and, as he inhales, he focuses his attention on the quality of the air entering his nostrils and he is saying to himself:

"I feel alert and refreshed. I am in control. I have done this before and it will go very well."

And, as he exhales, he is saying to himself:

"I feel relaxed and comfortable."

Our airline passenger has closed her eyes and is now shifting to slow abdominal breathing as she reclines in her seat. As she inhales, she focuses her attention on the air entering her nostrils and is saying to herself:

"I feel awake and alert and in control."

As she exhales slowly:

"I am relaxed and comfortable."

Such an exercise can also be used in other situations like a crowded elevator, when attending a stressful meeting, in a social setting, before engaging someone in a conversation, and before, during, or after any situation that creates enough anxiety to cause discomfort, anxiety, or panic.

The number of self-help stress-reduction books on bookstore shelves reminds us that many persons are now looking for relief. You may have previously sought help to either overcome your sense of failure at not becoming as socially or financially successful as you would have wished, or because you are now paying the cost of having achieved that success and of maintaining it in stress and physical symptoms.

Stress leading to anxiety, tension, and headaches can be more or less successfully controlled with prescription medication, including antianxiety sedatives and tranquilizers. But you may become dependent on them, and it has been reported that their long-term use may create a whole new set of problems, including thinking impairment.

That is one of the reasons that relaxation training, especially employing methods derived from meditation, has been so widely accepted as an alternate form of stress and anxiety reduction even among many traditional medical practitioners. The secret ingredient in all those techniques that have proved successful is diaphragmatic breathing. The most important component in meditation-type relaxation training is the naturally occurring reduction in breathing rate.[1]

The breathing methods described in this book are abstracted from ancient meditation techniques and refined to give you its essentials. Thus, when you are doing the breathing exercise, with or without the mental imagery, you are getting the *active* ingredients of meditation—the "wheat," as it were. I have taken great pains to refine it from the chaff.

There are two ways to use the breathing exercise: Either on a regular basis, two or three times per day, a triplet of rounds with imagery to reduce the general stress level, or in countertension, counteranxiety treatment, where you may wish to use the second set minus imagery.

Reducing the Frequency and Severity of Anxiety and Panic Attacks

Panic attacks and panic disorder with agoraphobia are so closely linked to hyperventilation that these two conditions are thought by many clinicians to be indistinguishable. This point is underscored by Dr. J. R. Marshall, professor of psychiatry at the University of Wisconsin Medical School.[2] The condition is characterized by breathing difficulty such as, "Can't catch my breath," "Can't get enough air" (dyspnea), palpitations, chest pain, and so on—that is, the criteria given in the DSM-IVR (see chapter 8).

It should be pointed out that an important aspect of the panic attack is that it is generally tied to the notion of imminent peril, such as that from a heart attack, from stroke, or from the likelihood of asphyxiation—in other words, the fear of dying.

Because of the relationship between panic attack and dyspnea— "Can't catch my breath!"—if you suffer from these disorders, I recommend that you attempt to make abdominal breathing habitual when at rest. This is not easy. First, you need to learn deep diaphragmatic breathing so that you can do its more subtle form on a regular basis. You can learn it in this book. I suggest that you proceed as indicated and do at least two sets of rounds each day.

Try to set a goal for yourself to remember to shift to diaphragmatic breathing for at least one or two breaths (without imagery)— not more—each time that you think of it during the course of the day. Reward yourself for remembering by saying to yourself, "Good! I remembered."

Do a set of rounds whenever you feel the beginning of an attack: As you do the breathing, say to yourself:

"It is not my heart. It is my breathing that makes me uncomfortable. As soon as I get my breathing under control, this attack will end. I can control it with my breathing."

Remember, a panic attack never lasts very long anyway. Time yours and see for yourself. They are self-limiting. And as your breathing improves, you may observe that even the frequency and duration of attacks will diminish.

Monitor the intake and reduce wheat, milk, sugar, coffee or tea, chocolate, or other foods that may trigger an anxiety or panic attack.

Tension Headache and TMJ

The term "tension headache" is something of a misnomer because it attributes headache to shoulder and neck muscle tension. In fact, in many cases it is quite the other way around—that is, headache causes tension. Here's why.

Most individuals know that muscle tension can cause discomfort and pain. Consequently, if they experience muscle tension and headache they may automatically assume that the tension came first and that it caused the headache. But the simple fact is that you cannot produce a headache simply by tensing the neck and shoulder muscles. Try it, you'll see what I mean. Headaches are invariably due to distention of blood vessels. That distention depends on blood-borne chemical substances, not on muscle tension.

But we also know that pain can cause a form of muscle bracing called *dysponesis*. In my experience with measuring the tension in the neck and shoulders of headache sufferers, I have found two sources of dysponetic bracing.

The first is the usual shoulder hunching and other skeletal muscle contraction that is common to pain in general. In the second, the typical headache sufferer will try to displace the head from an imagined spatial plane in which the pain is thought to be located. It is as if the patient is trying to move away from a location in the three-dimensional space that surrounds the head within which the pain actually is—like pulling your finger away from a hot lightbulb. This causes further and asymmetrical muscle tension. If you've ever suffered from bursitis of the elbow, did you find yourself trying (unsuccessfully) to move your arm around to find a place where it might not hurt quite as much?

Asymmetrical muscle tension is one of our most common sources of pain. It is typical in temporomandibular joint syndrome (TMJ) and bruxism (jaw clenching and teeth grinding).

For TMJ and bruxism, I also recommend frequent self-monitoring to help you to "tune in" to yourself. Just like the hyperventilation-related disorders, it is important to become conscious of the behavior that you wish to modify. You probably are not aware that you are tensing jaw muscles. Consequently, you may not think to relax them. So it is important to *think* about these things periodically and to ask yourself, "Am I clenching my jaws?"

Jaw clenching and teeth grinding are part of the muscle tension pattern that characterizes the way some persons react to the stresses of their life. TMJ is the pain in the jaw region associated with chronic contraction of the jaw muscles. Bruxism, for anyone who has ever wondered why his/her dentist bills were so high, is the grinding of teeth usually during sleep.

Breathing exercises are one of the most effective ways of relaxing and reducing muscle tension. For conditions that involve principally gross or skeletal muscles, you may find the use of the muscle relaxation exercises described in this book helpful as a prelude to doing the daily breathing exercises. I also recommend that you use the muscle relaxation exercises, coupled with a set of breathing rounds without imagery, at those times of the day when tension is high, at home or in the office if possible.

If you do clench your jaws as part of your tension pattern, I also recommend the following exercise: sit stoop-shouldered, hands loosely at your sides, head limply forward, mouth slightly agape, and lower jaw slack. Try this for about one minute each time that you are aware that you are clenching your jaws.

It has been my experience that some cases of TMJ, even those so designated by your dentist, are in fact not due to stress-related tension. There are many instances when they are undetected dental or orthodontic problems, some involving the more or less natural realignment of the jaws as teeth shift to the midline—a universal naturally occurring aging phenomenon, by the way.

Lowering Blood Pressure and Helping the Heart

If you are in the care of a physician prescribing medication, you may have been advised also to control your weight and sodium intake and to get "stress management," perhaps counseling and "relaxation training." You are probably inclined to follow your doctor's instructions. Also, you have heard or read somewhere that meditation and relaxation, including "better breathing," have helped others, so you are willing to give it a try. You may also note that you sometimes seem slightly out of breath.

Your decision is actually quite sound. Dr. C. Patel, a British physician writing for the *Lancet*, has shown conclusively that many meditation methods are so effective in lowering blood pressure that a good percentage of clients may go off medication.[3] Deep abdominal breathing is the active ingredient in meditation that most immediately lowers blood pressure.

Procedure for the First and Second Weeks

To begin with, you will wish to track your pulse rate and blood pressure regularly. Naturally, you should do this when you are at rest. You may observe your pulse rate and blood pressure with an easy-to-use self-inflating digital device obtainable at your nearby drugstore. Such devices have been said to be sometimes imprecise. But the error, in my experience, tends to be less than that occurring when someone inexperienced uses the old-fashioned cuff-and-stethoscope and fingers-on-the-artery method.

Since blood pressure and pulse rate vary with tension and anxiety, you will wish to know what accounts for what you are observing: Is it stress? Is it nutritional? Is your sodium intake up, or potassium level down? Have you had a high tyramine-foods day? Either stress or foods will cause these things to happen.

For this reason, please turn to any of the suspect foods lists in

Table 2 Symptoms severity checklist.

Name: _____ Date: _____

Symptoms:
  1)   Mild ( ),   Moderate ( ),   Severe ( )
  2)   Mild ( ),   Moderate ( ),   Severe ( )
  3)   Mild ( ),   Moderate ( ),   Severe ( )
  4)   Mild ( ),   Moderate ( ),   Severe ( )

Frequency: _____/day; and during the last week: _____

the chapter on nutrition. Make a copy of the protocol form on page 92, and begin to track these foods in your diet.

Mark your blood pressure, taken once in the morning and once in the evening, right on the form. If you have begun to eliminate the foods that contain substances promoting arterial blood vessel con-

Table 3 Blood pressure. Indicate systolic blood pressure before vertical line, and diastolic after it, for each sample taken each day. And indicate the pulse rate obtained with each blood pressure sample in the space below.

Example: 125/78
          (82)

Sample:	Mon	Tue	Wed	Thu	Fri	Sat	Sun
1)	__/__	__/__	__/__	__/__	__/__	__/__	__/__
	( )	( )	( )	( )	( )	( )	( )
2)	__/__	__/__	__/__	__/__	__/__	__/__	__/__
	( )	( )	( )	( )	( )	( )	( )
3)	__/__	__/__	__/__	__/__	__/__	__/__	__/__
	( )	( )	( )	( )	( )	( )	( )
4)	__/__	__/__	__/__	__/__	__/__	__/__	__/__
	( )	( )	( )	( )	( )	( )	( )
5)	__/__	__/__	__/__	__/__	__/__	__/__	__/__
	( )	( )	( )	( )	( )	( )	( )

striction or increased blood pressure, compare your resting blood pressure to that before nutrition changes.

Beginning Week Three

Now add the breathing exercises, using the schedule set forth above. When you have developed the skill of deep abdominal breathing so that you can do it effortlessly, you may also begin to do a round as a preventive measure in situations such as the following:

- Before a meeting
- During or after a nerve-racking meeting or other event
- When the bus is late
- In a traffic tie-up
- Waiting in line at the bank
- When the children are fighting with each other
- When your neighbor's stereo or television volume is too loud
- When the report due is not coming along smoothly
- When the bank teller can't find your account
- When the airlines reservations clerk announces that the computers are down

I am sure that you have no difficulty identifying the situations in your life that cause you to experience aggravation, tension, anxiety, and stress. Identify and list them in a hierarchy, in descending order of their annoyance value, beginning with the most annoying:

1. _____

2. _____

3. _____

4. _____

5. _____

Get into the habit of doing a breathing round (four breaths or so before, during, or after any such situation).

Keep track of the foods you consume, your blood pressure, and pulse rate at least twice a day. It will help you to maintain the program when you see it succeed for you.

Raynaud's and Hyperhidrosis

Raynaud's disease and Raynaud's syndrome are characterized by painfully cold extremities due to constriction of the capillaries, particularly in the fingers and toes. The fingers and toes may take on a blotched, bluish, or whitish appearance. If you have this condition, you know that it is painful and that your hands and feet are usually cold, especially in the winter.

Raynaud's disease was conventionally treated with prescription medication and, in the extreme case, surgery. In large measure this treatment was based on the finding of a combination of autonomic nervous system dysfunction and abnormal capillary networks first observed in the fingernail fold.[4] But more recently, it was shown that hand warming with biofeedback could, in many instances, also help to relieve this painful condition.

In my experience, any condition that could be relieved by hand warming also yielded to a combination of breathing training and tyraminergic food reduction. This approach was successful in quite a number of my clients, including Caroline.

Caroline: Raynaud's Disease

Caroline is a professional violinist whose career is just beginning to take off. She has already given concerts in major recital halls worldwide, and she has received numerous excellent critical notices. But before each concert, Caroline agonizes over her cold fingers and fears that they will hamper her performance.

Caroline has Raynaud's disease, and no medical treatment has so far given her reliable relief without adverse side effects that could compromise her performance. The tension and anxiety preceding each performance tend to aggravate that condition, so she dons woolen mittens offstage, and she blows warm breath into them to try to warm her hands.

She was referred to me for biofeedback treatment, but we decided in consultation to implement a program of combined nutritional control and diaphragmatic breathing instead of the conventional biofeedback hand-warming procedure. This decision was based on the observation that she was a chronic hyperventilator and that her blood carbon dioxide level was sufficiently low so that it would cause her blood vessels to constrict even if she did not have Raynaud's disease.

In consultation with her physician, Caroline agreed to try to eliminate tyraminergic foods from her diet and we proceeded with breathing retraining. She was given a small handheld digital thermometer to monitor the effect of the strategy. By the eighth training session, Caroline informed me that she was now able to normalize her hand temperature before performing by raising it by as much as 12°F with just a few minutes of diaphragmatic breathing.

Breathing and Hand Temperature

There have been many recent media accounts of the use of temperature biofeedback in the treatment of various stress- and anxiety-related disorders, particularly headaches.

As noted earlier, feedback provides knowledge of results about the performance of a task. Biofeedback may involve an instrument indicating how you are doing at learning to control an involuntary body function, such as pulse rate or blood pressure. The instrument can be as simple as a thermometer that can indicate when the arterial blood vessels in your skin are constricted.

When arterial blood vessels constrict, they limit blood flow in surrounding tissue and there is usually a corresponding drop in skin temperature. Skin temperature is measured at the surface of the skin—unlike body temperature, which is taken with a conventional thermometer. Intuitively you would expect your hand temperature to be warmer in a warm room than in a cool one. Hand temperature can only be an approximation of the temperature of blood flowing through the skin below the thermometer because it will also factor in room temperature. So, let's look at some simple guidelines.

At room temperature, about 70°F, you would expect hand temperature to be well above 87° to 88°F. Anything less suggests tension, stress, anxiety, or something else—maybe Raynaud's. I saw one young lady with a hand temperature of 76°F in a room at 78°F.

These people will laughingly tell you that they are famous for having the coldest hands anywhere: "My husband always says, 'Charlotte, don't touch me with your hands or feet when we go to bed!'"

Temperature biofeedback is frequently suggested to control these conditions. Self-regulation by trial and error with knowledge of results, one of the more common forms of biofeedback, is based on the assumption that learning to increase hand temperature improves blood flow through the hand and, therefore, through the body as a whole.

This assumption, though not accurate in its details, is not without considerable merit and research support. It has been shown to be very helpful in many cases. I have used it regularly with my clients, but with a twist, as you will see.

The typical procedure in temperature biofeedback is to provide you with a thermometer that has an attachment at the end of a wire that can be taped to one of your fingers. I recommend the home use of a simple digital thermometer with one-tenth of a degree steps, ranging at least from 70° to 100°F, which can be purchased at any hobby shop or hardware store. To observe your hand temperature, tape the little probe to your finger and wait for the temperature to stabilize.

Room and finger temperature may be noted, and you are then given minimal instructions to increase your finger temperature. Typically, learning progresses by trial and error, which you may spontaneously recognize to correspond to muscle relaxation.

Here's the twist: Arterial blood vessel diameter and therefore blood flow is also determined by the concentration of carbon dioxide in your blood. If you are hyperventilating, you are reducing your blood carbon dioxide level and your arteries will constrict. And so it

Table 4 Record each sample of your hand temperature, taken at the right index finger.

Example: (84.5) [degrees Fahrenheit]

	Mon	Tue	Wed	Thu	Fri	Sat	Sun
Room temp:	____	____	____	____	____	____	____
1)	( )	( )	( )	( )	( )	( )	( )
Room temp:	____	____	____	____	____	____	____
2)	( )	( )	( )	( )	( )	( )	( )
Room temp:	____	____	____	____	____	____	____
3)	( )	( )	( )	( )	( )	( )	( )
Room temp:	____	____	____	____	____	____	____
4)	( )	( )	( )	( )	( )	( )	( )
Room temp:	____	____	____	____	____	____	____
5)	( )	( )	( )	( )	( )	( )	( )

stands to reason that if you breathe properly you will correct blood carbon dioxide, which will relieve impaired circulation. As the correction takes place, you should be able to observe your hand temperature increasing.

This is very precisely what my clients observe during breathing retraining. Here is a simple way you can do it yourself.

Using that small digital handheld thermometer, tape the probe to your right index finger. Let the temperature stabilize. Record a sample of your hand temperature taken at the right index finger. Example: 84.5°F. Do not attempt this in a cold room where the temperature is well below 70°F.

Then do three diaphragmatic breathing rounds, each consisting of three consecutive inhale and exhale breath cycles, but separate each of these rounds with a one-minute pause. Now, note the hand temperature after the three rounds. You may wish to do this once in the morning and once in the evening, and you may wish to try it if you have a symptom episode.

It is desirable to record the temperature change from before the breathing exercise rounds and after doing them. That way, you can chart your progress and determine at what pace you are learning to warm your hands and whether that progress is giving you any degree of symptom relief.

You may also wish to bear in mind that you will benefit from simultaneously watching your food regimen. Tyramine-containing foods will lower the threshold for an attack and worsen anxiety by increasing arousal. It is difficult to slow things down that are speeded up by ideas when the body is independently speeded up. So monitor common foods, especially sugar, wheat, corn, milk, and MSG. You may be surprised to find that your hands are colder, your symptoms are worse, and that you feel worse on the days when you consume these foods.

This combination of hand warming and food control is equally applicable to Raynaud's syndrome, migraine, and idiopathic seizures, even though these conditions do not obviously form a homogeneous grouping. But they are so combined because of their dependence on factors affecting the blood vessels and oxygen delivery to body and brain tissues. The common factor, arterial constriction and spasms, differentiates them only with respect to the location of the arteries involved and has been elaborately described in previous sections to be a function of low oxygen (hypoxia).

Hyperhidrosis—Too Much Sweat: Stephanie and Sweating the Small Stuff

Hyperhidrosis is excessive perspiration due to overactivity of sweat glands. Many persons so afflicted are so embarrassed by it that it may cause them severe emotional distress. Until recently, treatment consisted mostly of the application of antiperspirants, though in severe cases oxybutynin (Ditropan) may be prescribed.

Stephanie was a twenty-seven-year-old woman with a fifteen-year history of hyperhidrosis, Raynaud's disease, and migraine headaches. She had been fully evaluated by numerous medical specialists over the last few years, and she was found to also suffer from other medical conditions including multiple allergies, sinusitis, cystitis, and eczema.

Stephanie was referred to me by her physician, who told me that all treatments had failed and that maybe reducing her chronic stress levels might help her. But the observation that she often had exceptionally cold hands at normal room temperatures, coupled with the fact that prescription medications are usually antispasmodic, led me to consider a connection between her hyperhidrosis and her Raynaud's disease.

She began breathing training and, in cooperation with her physician, she was given a small digital thermometer with which to observe her hand temperature at indicated times. She was also immediately instructed to keep a daily before- and after-each-meal food and hand-temperature diary, and to scrupulously avoid tyraminergic foods such as those listed in chapter 5.

Conforming to a regular schedule of breathing exercises and identifying hand-cooling food substances and eliminating them from her daily diet had the net effect of improving peripheral blood circulation. Her hand temperature gradually rose to normal levels, and by the end of the seventh week of treatment Stephanie reported that her hyperhydrosis was now minimal, without any additional medication.

Migraine and Seizure Disorders

In migraine, nausea and vomiting, as well as sensory disturbances of vision, hearing, or smell may be the only symptoms, or these may precede pain in the head or abdomen.

I have treated a number of persons with migraine and idiopathic (of unknown origin) epileptic seizures—one even with seizures with a medical cause—who were able to avert or abort migraine or seizures if they began deep abdominal breathing as soon as they experienced the premonitory signs.

Consequently, I also recommend that a set of three abdominal breathing rounds, four to five breaths with no imagery, with two to three minutes rest between rounds, be used when premonitory symptoms appear.

You may note that if you do this properly, your hands will feel warmer as their temperature will rise considerably.

Elimination of the migraine foods listed in the previous chapter has been very helpful to many of my clients. Watch out for common foods with high concentrations of the amino acids tyramine, tyrosine, or tryptophan. And keep in mind that the first successful treatment of seizure conditions was nutritional—the ketogenic diet (ketones are produced in the metabolism of fat). This is the same diet recommended by Dr. Atkins for weight loss!

Watch especially sugar, red meat, wine, wheat, milk, corn, licorice, spinach, MSG, and fried foods. And remember, hypoglycemia is well known to increase the frequency and severity of these conditions. Lower your sodium intake.

It is also advisable to monitor hand temperature as a good indicator of threshold. As previously noted, I have seen clients in these disorder categories whose hand temperature was well below room temperature. You may notice, if you suffer any one of these conditions, your hand temperature tells the tale.

If you are able to eliminate tyraminergic foods from your diet without impairing nutrition, you will notice very quickly that your typical hand temperature will increase considerably. As you note the increase in hand temperature, you should also begin to see a decrease in the frequency and/or the severity of your symptoms. Careful tracking of symptoms will show you that objectively.

Then, when you begin to add abdominal breathing to your routine, you may notice a further increase in average hand temperature and a further decrease in symptom severity and frequency.

When you have mastered abdominal breathing, you may note a rapid increase in hand temperature—just from the breathing change!

A concerted effort should be made to shift permanently to abdominal breathing when at rest—and especially to control any spontaneously initiated hyperventilation—because migraine and seizures are very sensitive to the effects of low blood carbon dioxide.

Reducing Menopausal Hot Flashes

There are very few conditions that can be treated with breathing training that were *directly* caused by improper breathing, but many factors need to be present before a disorder emerges. By the same token, there are very few conditions that proper breathing will cure. And I do not claim otherwise.

But most disorders are significantly aggravated by improper breathing. And most disorders are significantly ameliorated by restoring proper breathing. In fact, I use a short form of the breathing exercise to raise my threshold for pain at the dentist—until the anesthetic takes effect.

Any new application of breathing training to reduce human suffering merits attention. In this connection, I cite its recent application to reducing menopausal hot flashes.

Doctors Freedman and Woodward reported that by using measures of changes in the skin, which reliably correspond to verbal reports of flashes experienced by menopausal women, a group taught paced-respiration had a significant decrease in hot flashes as their breathing rate declined, while a muscle relaxation group showed neither breathing rate decline nor reduced hot flashes. The authors concluded that "training in a simple breathing procedure results in a significant reduction in menopausal hot flushes [sic.] as measured over a twenty-four-hour period. This technique may be useful for women with hot flushes who are unable to receive hormone replacement therapy."[5]

This is a very exciting finding and I hope that other innovative applications will follow it. But I would choose the diaphragmatic breathing training method described in this book over paced-respiration as a method of breath control.

In paced breathing, the client is given a means of controlling his or her breathing rate either by counting or by using a metronome or other such "rhythm pacing" means. Pacing is an artificial way of slowing down breathing and does not allow the client to find his or her natural optimum breathing pattern. However, it is noteworthy that even pacing breathing produces a result.

Gastritis and Diabetes

Gastrointestinal disorders are thought to be strongly influenced by stress. Diabetes can also be added to this category. But there is no evidence that these conditions are actually caused by stress, nor by psychological or emotional disorders. Quite the contrary.

Medicine now knows that gastritis can result from a multitude of different causes, ranging from inadequate stomach acidity to adverse reaction to antibiotics and even aspirin. Ulcers are most often due to a bacterial infection (*Helicobacter pylori*). However, these conditions, as well as diabetes, are thought to be strongly *aggravated* by stress or emotion regardless of their cause.

Breathing

Clients with these disorders are usually referred to me for relaxation training and stress reduction. The reason for this is that most physicians are aware that the stress hormones have an adverse effect on these conditions. Consequently, they may recommend behavioral relaxation methods in accordance with their orientation.

Daily sets of breathing rounds, preceded by the muscle relaxation exercises, may be supplemented by the use of the exercise without imagery several times during the day. This takes, all in all, about fifteen minutes or so out of the day.

CAUTION: Research reports have shown that muscle relaxation can significantly reduce insulin dependence. If you are insulin dependent and you are doing deep-breathing and muscle relaxation exercises, consult with your physician and monitor blood sugar regularly.

Nutrition

Each of these conditions has special nutritional requirements which are beyond the scope of this book. But I would like to mention that it has been very helpful to keep the following in mind:

- Chromium, obtainable as a dietary supplement in drug- and health-food stores and taken under the direction of your physician, helps to stabilize the *glucose tolerance factor* (GTF) in diabetes and hypoglycemia. It may tend to reduce the dependence on insulin, so watch out.

- Any digestive problem resulting in malabsorption syndrome may result in significant potassium loss that will aggravate the condition further. Potassium has been shown to be essential in regulating digestion.

Ulcerative colitis and Crohn's disease have recently been shown to be autoimmune reactions to bacteria called *M. paratuberculosis* (this is not the conventional tuberculosis, but a different bacteria). Macrophages and lymphocytes of the immune system are sensitized to these bacteria, and in their effort to eradicate them they irritate the mucous lining of the digestive system.

Standard laboratory tests for the presence of these germs and the proper antibiotics have been shown to lead to proper treatment and to resolve the problem. But the disorder has also been shown to cause folic acid deficiency. Consequently, supplementation may be in order.

Insomnia: A Wonderful Breathing Exercise

Insomnia may be the inability to fall asleep, or it may be frequent waking during the night with an inability to fall asleep again. Insomnia is often the result of the inability to relinquish daytime tensions and concerns by nighttime. If you suffer from this debilitating condition, you may benefit from relaxation. Do the daily combination of muscle relaxation exercises and breathing exercises with imagery.

Using Abdominal Breathing to Help You Sleep

When you have mastered deep abdominal breathing by practicing the daily exercises for a few days or weeks, and you can do them easily and smoothly, you may proceed as shown below.

This exercise may be done sitting in your home, at the office, while traveling, or reclining in bed at night. It is a relaxation exercise which is *not* intended to produce alert relaxation. Although you would do it in bed if you intend to use it to help you to fall asleep, it can be done equally well sitting up. But let me illustrate its use as an aid to slumber.

First, read the instructions from beginning to end so that you can do them with your eyes closed. Then, as you are reclining in bed, make yourself comfortable, let the tension drain from your body, and begin to concentrate on abdominal breathing:

Inhale . . . fill up. Good. Now, as you exhale, say to yourself:

"I'm letting the tension out of my forehead."

Focus your attention on your forehead. Pull back your abdomen gently, on exhale. That's good. Inhale again . . . and, as you exhale, say to yourself:

"I'm letting the tension in my forehead flow out with my breath."

Focus your attention on the tension in your forehead, feel it flowing out with your breath. You inhale again . . . and as you exhale, say:

"I'm letting the tension out of my face. I'm letting my jaws relax."

Focus your attention on your face and jaws. Inhale . . . fill up. That's good. As you exhale, say to yourself:

"I'm letting the tension in my face and jaws drift out with my breath."

Feel the tension flowing out with your breath. Next, exhale again, and as you exhale, say to yourself:

"I'm letting the tension out of my neck and out of my shoulders. I'm letting my shoulders down."

Focus your attention on your neck . . . your shoulders. Then inhale again, and as you exhale, say to yourself:

"I'm letting the tension in my neck and my shoulders flow out with my breath."

Get a sense that you can feel the tension in your neck and shoulders flow out with your breath as you exhale.

Next, inhale . . . and as you exhale, if you are lying in bed, first imagine that the weight in your arms is drifting to their underside, that is, the part of your arms resting on the bed. Focus your attention on your arms and your hands and say to yourself:

"I'm letting the tension out of my arms and out of my hands and my arms feel heavy."

Inhale fully. Good. Now exhale and say to yourself:

"I'm letting the tension flow out with my breath."

As you focus your attention on your arms and hands, feel it flow out.

Inhale. Exhale, and if you are lying in bed, first get a sense that the weight in your body is drifting to the underside of your body—the side in contact with the bed—and say to yourself:

"I'm letting the weight in my body drift to the underside of my body."

Inhale. Exhale and say to yourself:

"I'm letting the tension in my body flow out with my breath."

Get a sense that the tension in your body is flowing out with your breath.

Good night.

If you are doing this exercise in a sitting position, your feet are flat on the floor before you. Instead of saying, "I'm letting the weight in my body drift to the underside of my body," substitute, "I'm letting myself sink further back into the seat, letting the seat support my weight, and I'm letting the weight in my body drift to the bottom of my feet."

Nutrition

There are many substances that will contribute to restlessness, and some that will help you to fall asleep. Stimulants such as sugar and caffeine will promote sleeplessness. So will tyramine in foods, chocolate, tea, coffee, and colas (which often contain caffeine). They promote rapid pulse rate and palpitations, among other signs. Many also contain salicylates (in additives and coloring), which contribute to hyperactivity in some children (see the list in chapter 10).

Some foods contain substances that actually promote sleep: tryptophan, found in abundance in milk and turkey, for example, helps you to fall asleep. Bear in mind, however, that milk is mucogenic (promotes mucus) and may cause snoring or promote hyperventilation during sleep by blocking the air passages of the nose. It is always a trade-off. Even though tryptophan is a nutrient substance, it may promote headaches in those so predisposed.

Seymour: Anxiety

Seymour is a thirty-two-year-old single man employed in the fashion industry. He is of average height and weight. As he entered my office, his gait and posture suggested weariness, perhaps even depression. His handshake was weak and his hand was cool.

He reported suffering from "panic attacks" which occurred principally when he traveled. The disorder is in quotes here because I did not agree with his assertion. His description was better suited to anxiety attacks with a mild agoraphobia. The attacks did not have many of the characteristics of typical panic attacks.

He expressed some doubt at first about how the breathing exercises would help him with his symptoms. I explained the relationship between anxiety and tension and told him that breathing training would facilitate a "relaxation response" that would help him. His breathing rate was 21 b/min and his carbon dioxide was 4.82 percent. After the third weekly abdominal breathing training session, his breathing rate dropped to 4 b/min during training.

On the fourth session, Seymour reported that his anxiety was considerably reduced and that he could control his attacks on public transportation by switching to abdominal breathing. After the fifth session, he had one session every two weeks, and after the ninth session, he felt confident that he could continue on his own.

Stress-related and psychophysiological disorders have in common mechanisms reflected in breathing. I have found that relaxation training centering on slow, deep, abdominal breathing has been enormously helpful to most of my clients whose complaints and symptoms span a wide range of stress-related and psychophysiological disorders. I recommend it, together with other treatment strategies, including nutrition, to strengthen the ability of your body to fight back.

PART THREE

How Breathing Is Connected to Specific Health Disorders

CHAPTER 7

Breathing, Hypertension, and the Heart

The Pulse Story

Let's assume that you are a relatively healthy professional man or woman in your mid forties. It's been a routine day at the office and traffic was not exceptionally dense on your return home. Now it is evening and you've enjoyed a pleasant dinner with your family. You're sitting comfortably in your favorite chair now and you are reading or watching television. The major feature on the dinnertime news concerns a banal mayoral address to a local civic club. You do not smoke.

You might expect your pulse rate to be between 70 and 80 beats per minute and your blood pressure to be about 135/75 mm Hg. Your breathing rate would be around 12 to 14 breaths per minute (b/min).

But now, let's suppose that you are sitting (and slowly sinking) into a soft leather couch in the waiting room of the executive suite of your firm. The surroundings may best be described as posh: senseless but obviously costly wall decorations and art objects have been dispersed strategically around the room to give the impression of class.

A receptionist in fashionable drab, not a hair out of place, sits behind a rosewood desk and shunts incoming phone calls to various department heads—all vice presidents of the company, a position to which you aspire (note the breathing-related meaning of this term). This position is as precariously dependent on continuous high-level performance as that of a stunt pilot (with about equal casualty rates).

In spite of your best efforts, *The Report*, which is your responsibility, is woefully inadequate. You have for some time been trying to avoid facing the fact that, because of lack of time and inadequate resources, there are gaps and errors throughout. So your department head, a man who has gone on record as stating that tact and goodwill are signs of weakness, has requested that you meet with him.

While you are sitting there and estimating the likelihood of finding other suitable employment in the geographic region in which your children attend school, it might not be unreasonable to suppose that your calm and composed appearance masks tension and anxiety.

Your blood pressure may rise to 165/95, and your pulse rate to 110. Your breathing rate may reach 18 or more per minute even though no one else would be aware of that. However, you heave occasional deep sighs.

As time goes by, your hands begin to feel cold and clammy. You begin to fidget with the folder on your lap, and you can feel your chest pounding. You start at the dreaded, though expected, sound of "Mr./Ms. Smith? Mr. Jones will see you now."

How Breathing Affects Your Cardiovascular System

The way you breathe, how fast you breathe, the rhythm of your inhale and exhale cycles, and whether you breathe predominantly with your chest or abdomen have a profound effect on your cardiovascular system, meaning your heart, arteries, and blood vessels. Breathing can increase or decrease the diameter of your blood vessels, your blood pressure, and the work output of your heart (stroke volume). Breathing also affects the timing of the heart beats—its own pacemaker rhythm.

The most commonly observed breathing disorder associated with stress or psychophysiological disorders is rapid, shallow chest breathing with hyperventilation. Disordered breathing can significantly raise blood pressure and pulse rate, but breathing control is an effective adjunct to normalizing these functions and, in some cases, the best method to control them.

Predictable changes in arterial blood pressure occur principally as a function of respiration rate: When breathing is within the normal range, your blood pressure will fall slightly during inspiration. But when doing slow diaphragmatic breathing, your arterial blood pressure will drop slightly with pulse rate during expiration.

When you hyperventilate, blood circulation increases to the large skeletal muscles while blood flow to the hands, feet, and brain decreases. That is one of the reasons for doing slow diaphragmatic breathing during a migraine attack: it restores blood circulation to the extremities. Many migraine sufferers are notorious for their frequently cold extremities, and hand warming with breathing exercises and so-called autosuggestion has been shown to be effective in relieving those symptoms.

Just as breathing affects blood pressure, blood pressure may also affect breathing. Within limits, blood flow through the head may vary with blood pressure in the body, but blood flow through the brain decreases as breathing rate increases because, as breathing becomes more rapid, blood concentration of carbon dioxide decreases, causing brain arteries to constrict.

This relationship between breathing and blood pressure seems somehow to have been forgotten nowadays. Yet it has been known for a very long time; it was summarized in a little book intended for physicians, titled *The Cure of High Blood Pressure by Respiratory Exercises*, first published in the late 1920s.[1] That relationship boils down to this: Elevated blood pressure accompanies those bodily states where rapid, shallow breathing prevails. By altering breathing to a slow diaphragmatic mode, blood pressure decreases.

Elevated blood pressure is a major American health problem. According to a 1998 report in the *New York Times*, citing the National Center for Health Statistics as its source, about half of middle-aged

Americans have elevated blood pressure. Women have a slightly higher blood pressure.[2]

Blood is known to all of us as that dark red liquid in our arteries and veins. It consists of the fluid plasma, which contains different types of "formed" cells (formed means having a solid form or shape), some red and round, others white and irregular, circulating in blood vessels throughout the body and under pressure from the pumping action of the heart. Among the round cells are the red blood cells, which contain hemoglobin and transport oxygen and carbon dioxide about the body, and the blood platelets, which serve to plug up leaks should they occur in blood vessels. The white cells are typically immune system lymphocytes, more or less spherical in shape, and irregularly shaped macrophages that help clean up debris.

Most experts and lay persons alike today still think of blood simply as a body fluid, not as a living tissue. It is rarely emphasized that a tissue does not have to be solid. A tissue is defined as one or more types of cells, usually assembled into a unit that performs a specific biological function.

Oxygenated blood flows from the lungs and back into the body through the left side of the heart, via the aorta, the largest artery trunk in the body. The arteries, made up of an endothelium cell lining surrounded by adjoining smooth muscle rings, narrow to arterioles and then to capillaries, which are only one cell thick and have no surrounding smooth muscle rings.

As blood courses through the capillaries, some of which have a diameter less than that of a single red blood cell, it gives up much of its oxygen and nutrients to surrounding tissues, organs, and muscles, and takes on carbon dioxide and other waste products. But it can only do so if there is sufficient pressure to help it through the capillaries and into the veins for the return trip to the lungs, via the right side of the heart.

There are numerous physiological factors that affect the strength and the rate of contraction of the heart, and the diameter of arteries, arterioles, and capillaries. These include the action of physiological pressure regulator, chemical and other hormone mechanisms, and neurotransmitters such as norepinephrine, acetylcholine, and (it has recently been discovered) the gas nitric oxide. All of these, interacting in various combinations, result in your blood pressure at any given moment.

You can readily feel rhythmic blood pressure pulses in arteries at various points on your body. The wrist is a favorite place to "take" the pulse. You have seen your physician do this many times. With your hand positioned palm up, the index and middle fingers of your opposite hand are placed across your wrist over the radial artery. The pulsations may be timed to give you pulse in beats per minute. There is one pulse for each contraction of the heart. In normal adults at rest, pulse rate will vary between about seventy and eighty beats per minute.

The heart is a fist-shaped muscle, weighing about one pound and containing two synchronized pumps—one on the right side and one on the left. Each pump consists of two chambers which recirculate your total blood volume—an average of about five quarts. Ordinarily, this is accomplished under the control of its own automatic pacemakers located in the sinoatrial and atrioventricular nodes, which determine the rate and patterns of its contractions.

During the course of an average day, your heart will beat over 100,000 times and pump about 1,800 gallons of blood at a rate of about 70 beats per minute. Quite an undertaking for a fist-sized muscle!

Your heart contractions are triggered by a tiny electrical current. This can be picked up by little electrode pads on your chest and amplified. This forms the basis for the electrocardiogram (ECG), which indicates which phase of the contraction of the heart is in progress. Some components of this current are the trigger to the heart muscle to contract, while others are the result of the muscle contraction itself.

Cardiac arrhythmias are deviations in this electrical signal resulting from changes in the activity of the heart musculature. They may reflect minor changes in the concentration of essential substances called electrolytes that facilitate the flow of an electric current through an otherwise nonconducting muscle medium. These include sodium, calcium, magnesium, and potassium. Or they may represent life-threatening conditions.

The strength of the contraction of your heart—in a sense, the change in its size—determines the amount of blood it will pump through your arteries with each contraction. It is the major factor in *systolic blood pressure:* systole is the contraction phase and diastole is the relaxation phase of the activity of the heart.

The rate and the volume pumped with each beat are determined by many different factors. The major ones are the metabolic demands made by activity, the stimulation of the heart by the sympathetic branch of the autonomic nervous system through the release of the action hormones (adrenaline and noradrenaline) into the blood, the influence of stimulation by a nerve called the vagus, signals from various body pressure receptors, the health of the heart muscle, and whether one exercises regularly and maintains a proper balance of nutrients and minerals.

How Breathing Affects Your Pulse Rate

Pulse rate appears to be regular in most persons. Heartbeats appear to be more or less regularly spaced over time. Actually, in persons who are breathing normally, pulse rate can significantly rise with inspiration and drop with expiration.

Because it is relatively uncommon to observe this pattern in most persons, medicine erroneously called it *respiratory sinus arrhythmia* (RSA). It is in no sense of the word an indication of a disorder. In fact, it is most pronounced in children (before they learn to breathe with their chest), in athletes, and in persons who have learned slow, abdominal breathing.

It has been my common experience that my clients almost never show RSA before breathing retraining, and show a restoration of that pattern after they learn to control their breathing. In fact, I use an RSA cycling over six to nine beats per minute as an indication of improvement.

In 1732, the English physiologist Stephen Hales severed an artery in the leg of a horse and inserted a slender glass tube into it. He observed that the blood escaping from the artery rose in the glass tube to a height of over eight feet above the heart of the animal. Fortunately we don't measure blood pressure quite that way anymore—we use an indirect method.

Blood pressure is ordinarily observed with a pressure cuff. The cuff is usually placed over your left bicep muscle, about two inches above your elbow. It is then inflated until the pressure stops the blood flowing in the brachial artery.

A stethoscope is then placed over that artery and air is slowly released from the cuff until a strong thumping sound is heard. This sound indicates restoration of blood flow through the artery. The pressure at which this sound is heard is the *systolic blood pressure.*

As air continues to escape from the cuff, the sound fades. The pressure at the point where it disappears indicates the *diastolic pressure.* Although there is some degree of normal variation in the average person at rest, the ratio of the systolic and diastolic pressures should be about 135/75 millimeters of mercury (mm Hg), respectively or, as they say, "135 over 75."

The French physiologist Claude Bernard was the first to show, in the mid-nineteenth century, that the diameter of arteries is strongly influenced by the autonomic nervous system. Subsequently we have learned that the medulla in the brain is largely responsible for transmission of nerve impulses to blood vessels. Messages from all parts of the body—but especially from the carotid sinus in the neck, the arch of the aorta after it exits from the left ventricle of the heart, the respiratory centers of the medulla itself, as well as countless hormones that directly regulate arteries and body fluid level—modify the circulatory system.

When Hales first observed the blood pressure in the artery of a horse, he also noted that it rose and fell, apparently in synchrony with respiration. In persons breathing normally, blood pressure alternately rises and falls slightly with inspiration and expiration.

How Your Arteries Relax and Constrict

The activity of the brain center (the medulla), which controls the diameter of your arteries, is affected by the concentration of carbon dioxide circulating in your arterial blood. This concentration is, in turn, affected directly by breathing. When carbon dioxide concentration is normal, the diameter of the arteries is normal and blood circulation is unimpeded. But when carbon dioxide is below normal, the arteries constrict, reducing their diameter, and blood pressure rises as blood flow is impeded.

The same thing happens to arteries and blood circulation in the brain when blood carbon dioxide concentration changes, but there is one major way that it differs from body arteries. In the body, the diameter of the vessels is also under the control of the autonomic nervous system; but in the brain, the diameter of the arteries forming the so-called vascular bed is determined almost entirely by the concentration of carbon dioxide in circulating blood. The autonomic nervous system has been shown to have no direct effect on the diameter of brain arteries and arterioles; sympathetic autonomic nervous system stimulation does not cause dilation of brain arteries.

When you hyperventilate, you may shortly feel dizzy and faint. If you keep this up, you may even pass out. Several mechanisms combine simultaneously to produce this effect. First, loss of carbon dioxide results in narrowing of brain arteries, reducing blood flow to the brain. There follows a precipitous drop in oxygen to the brain (at this point, your brain waves may show the same general pattern as that found during a seizure). In addition, blood pressure may suddenly reverse the upward trend and drop dramatically.

You may wonder why one would expect to see decreased blood pressure in hyperventilation when it has been repeatedly shown to be associated with high blood pressure. The hyperventilation that is observed in chronic tension and anxiety is associated, in the long run, with high blood pressure, because that form of hyperventilation reflects the driving effects of sympathetic autonomic nervous system activity. But when a person is breathing more or less normally, and is then instructed to breathe quickly, as in the hyperventilation challenge, blood pressure is usually observed to drop markedly. As previously noted, the impairment in circulation may be sufficient to create a health risk.

How Hyperventilation Can Affect the Heart

Doctors Evans and Lum alerted us in *Practical Cardiology* to different types of chest pain in hyperventilation.[3] And the journal *Chest* described in detail the three major types of chest pain experienced by persons when hyperventilating:

- Sharp, fleeting, periodic, originating in the anterior left chest, radiating into the neck, left scapula (shoulder blade), and along the inferior rib margins. Intensity is increased by deep breathing, twisting, and bending.
- Persistent, localized aching discomfort, usually under the left breast (lasting for hours or even for days, not varying in intensity with activity or motion of chest wall). Chest wall is tender at the site of the pain (a local anesthetic provides relief).
- Diffuse, dull, aching, heavy pressure sensation over the entire precordium or substernum which does not vary with respiration activity (may last for minutes or days and is often confused with angina).[4]

Angina and pseudoangina (Prinzmetal's variant form), have been reported by numerous clinicians in connection with hyperventilation. Some concluded that hyperventilation is a precipitating factor in all forms of angina and angina-like symptoms.

The mechanisms implicated in these symptoms are related to reduced blood flow to the heart tissues and low oxygen content of the blood. In fact, an article in the journal *Postgraduate Medicine* refers to cardiac manifestations of hyperventilation as "mimics of coronary heart disease."[5]

Systematic investigation of the electrocardiogram in hyperventilation has revealed a number of common signs. But their significance is debated. It has been my experience that clients with "skipped beats" and other forms of trace abnormality have been told by their physicians that these are essentially benign. Yet there is some evidence to the contrary.

A report in the *Journal of Clinical Investigation* concludes that electrocardiographic changes are highly indicative of the fact that the heart is not getting enough oxygen.[6]

Medical investigators reported the outcome of their study of the breathing patterns found in heart attack patients in *The Research Bulletin of the Himalayan International Society* (devoted to holistic health). They described these patterns for 153 patients in the critical care unit of a hospital in Minneapolis-St. Paul. The breathing patterns were found to consist of predominantly chest breathing in patients with myocardial infarction; 76 percent showed mouth breathing.[7]

Larry: Hypertension

Larry is a forty-one-year-old married securities broker with three children. His medical history reveals nothing out of the ordinary. He drinks occasionally at social gatherings and does not smoke, but though he watches his diet and exercises regularly at a health club, he suffers moderate hypertension.

Initially, his breathing rate was 22 b/min, and his carbon dioxide was 5.84 percent. The latter is significantly elevated, indicating that even while sitting in my recliner, he was "spinning his wheels rapidly." His blood pressure was 142/95.

He quickly learned deep abdominal breathing and when coupled with beach imagery was able to bring his breathing under control in fifteen minutes. His breathing rate dropped to 4.75 b/min and his carbon dioxide normalized to 4.94 percent, while his blood pressure dropped to 138/83.

Larry comes in every few weeks to check his progress and practice his breathing exercise under my supervision. His blood pressure continues to decline and is now in the 130/80 range.

Victor: Hypertension and Hyperventilation

Victor is a thirty-two-year-old professional. He is married and has no children. Well above average in height and of athletic build, he came to see me because of borderline hypertension. In addition, he reported mild tension associated with his work schedule, but otherwise appeared to be in good health.

His breathing rate was found to be 18 b/min with carbon dioxide (3.92 percent) well below the normal limit of about 4.75 percent for a person with his body build. This is a hyperventilation pattern. It came as a surprise to him that he was breathing predominantly with his chest—he'd just never thought about it.

His blood pressure was initially 150/89 mm Hg. He was taught deep diaphragmatic breathing and, within minutes, his breathing rate dropped to 4.75 b/min with normalized carbon dioxide (4.88 percent). At that point, his blood pressure was 137/89 mm Hg.

After four once-per-week training sessions, his breathing dropped further to 3 b/min during training, with normal carbon dioxide (4.98 percent), and his blood pressure went from 133/75 mm Hg before the breathing exercise to 126/72 mm Hg after it. After the fourth session, there was no further need to see me and he terminated treatment.

Marvin: "Harmless" Arrhythmia?

Marvin is a forty-five-year-old contractor. He is married and has two children. He came to see me at the insistence of his psychotherapist because of his many "psychosomatic" symptoms. He is slightly above average in height, and well built. He was dressed in a suit, entered my office briskly, spoke clearly and to the point. Although he gave no outward indication of it by his manner or posture, he reported chronic fatigue, tension, anxiety, a mild depression, and, in general, stress.

His medical symptoms included airborne and food allergies, and skipped heartbeats which had been identified for him as ventricular premature contractions (VPC). Parenthetically, a number of my clients have this condition, which is described to them by their physicians as a "harmless" arrhythmia. But to panic sufferers who feel the skipped beat, this is not reassuring at all.

At the initial evaluation, his breathing rate was found to be 12 b/min and his carbon dioxide was elevated to 5.67 percent. I thought at the time that this was an inconsistent observation and made a point to make a note of it. If his carbon dioxide was that elevated, his breathing rate should have been elevated also as part of an accelerated metabolic reaction. Carbon dioxide elevates only with normal breathing when the individual had previously low blood carbon dioxide due to hyperventilation.

Subsequently, it turned out that Marvin thought that he should slow down his breathing so that he would "look good on the test." Inspection of the computer tracing shows quite clearly a slow exhale with a rapid, gasplike inhale—not even a common *unnatural* pattern. The pulse tracing showed irregular heartbeats (VPCs).

Marvin has been in training now for twenty-one sessions. His breathing is under control, at about 3 to 4 b/min when he is doing slow abdominal breathing exercises. He is much improved and his anxiety and tension are greatly reduced. Curiously, the VPCs are mostly gone, except on very bad allergy days. His allergies likewise lessened following medical nutritional adjustment.

Things to Do

Self-monitoring of blood pressure by itself is rarely an indication that you are overconcerned with your health (i.e., that you are a hypochondriac). Most ordinary people monitor all sorts of things, including their daily sodium intake, their caloric intake, and their weight. Most sources recommend that you monitor your consumption of vitamins, minerals, and antioxidants. Blood pressure should be monitored regularly. Any of the conventional inflate/deflate, cuff-over-the-arm types that can be obtained in your neighborhood drugstore may be adequate to the task.

You might wish to keep a record of morning and evening blood pressure for two weeks so that you will have a baseline against which you can then periodically check and see if there is any significant change.

CHAPTER 8

Breathing Problems, Anxiety, and Depression

Melancholoke folke are commonly given to sigh, because the minde being possessed with great varietie and store of foolish apparitions doth not remember or suffer the partie to be at leisure to breathe according to the necessitie of nature.
—Dulaurens, 1559

Alex: Panic Disorder

Last Wednesday, at about one o'clock in the afternoon, Alex waited patiently on the platform of a New York subway station, staring down the tracks to see the approaching train. It was an ordinary day. There was absolutely nothing special about this trip that he was making to visit a friend, and he could not recall having had any disturbing feelings at all.

In a few moments the train appeared, the doors of the car facing Alex opened, and passengers emerged. People waiting on the crowded platform began to enter the car. And so did Alex.

As was customary at that time of day, Alex readily found a seat and he hunkered down for the trip. Although most of the seats in the car were occupied, the car was far from crowded now and there were only a few straphangers. The train began to leave the station.

A few minutes into the trip, Alex suddenly began to experience a strange feeling of breathlessness followed by lightheadedness. He

129

did not pay much mind to it at first, but it got perceptibly stronger and he found now that he couldn't catch his breath. He was choking, or so it seemed to him.

As the sensation grew in intensity Alex began to feel extremely anxious, and he wondered if other passengers could discern his discomfort. The anxiety now swelled into a silent terror as he felt his heart wildly pounding in his chest. He wondered if he were having a heart attack, and he felt an almost uncontrollable urge to try to escape from the train even though reason told him that it was still in motion, and that it would certainly come to a station momentarily.

When it appeared to Alex that the train was in the station, he prepared to bolt out the door. When the doors opened, he ran out of the car, up the station stairs, and into the street where he gasped for air and finally felt the beginnings of relief.

Alex had experienced his first panic attack.

The Breathing-Emotion Connection

The spirometer, an instrument that measures the volume of air and its pattern as it moves in and out of the lungs during respiration, was introduced in the 1930s, when it became fashionable to look at breathing in emotions. Scientists came to the conclusion that there were certain distinct types of "respiratory neuroses," specifically anxiety and hysteria. And they thought that these were essentially respiratory in nature. Think of it: scientists thought that anxiety could be brought about by faulty breathing. But even more remarkable was a series of studies that showed that stimulating breathing could even momentarily restore sanity in schizophrenic patients.[1]

The study of breathing did not constitute a coherent discipline until the 1950s, when the following observations of breathing patterns in persons with psychological disorders of the anxiety type were reported:

- inability to catch one's breath or get enough air (dyspnea)
- frequent sighing (sighing respiration)
- increased respiration rate (tachypnea or hyperpnea)

- irregularity of breathing (disturbance of inhalation/exhalation coordination)
- sharp transition between inhale and exhale
- prolonged inspiration and curtailed expiration
- principally thoracic respiration
- shallow respiration
- inspiratory shift of median position

Based on these observations, it was suggested that a number of technical measures of breathing, such as the ratio of the duration of inspiration to expiration, might be useful in the assessment of anxiety because:

- Anxious women use a smaller part of the respiration cycle for inspiration than do anxious men.
- Anxious men have a significantly more rapid respiration than do normal men (16 versus 11 b/min).
- In anxious men and women, a larger part of the respiration cycle is employed for expiration in abdominal breathing than in thoracic breathing.[2]

It was also reported that normal men breathe more slowly than normal women, but that sex differences disappear in the breathing patterns of anxious men and women. Finally, another study reported that the highest abnormal spirometer readings were found in persons with anxiety.[3]

What do these studies tell us? First, that there are objective, scientific measures of breathing. And second, that they can be used reliably to differentiate breathing patterns in persons suffering anxiety from those not so afflicted. Breathing pattern alone may be a reliable indication of anxiety level.

You might well say, "But, breathing reflects arousal, doesn't it? Isn't that what you pointed out before?" And I would answer you this way: "It isn't simply a matter of breathing rate—how quickly you breathe. It is a matter of other aspects of the pattern, including the relative duration of the inspiration and expiration."

Others have reported additional measures of breathing that show clearly that specific respiratory changes accompany different mental states and emotions, especially anxiety. For instance, the rate, or depth, of breathing increases, and sighing increases mostly with anxiety but sometimes when one experiences anger or resentment. The breathing rate decreases when one is tense or vigilant. Breathing may become especially irregular when anger is suppressed.

Breathing and Depression

Breathing changes in people suffering from depression have been reported in the *British Journal of Psychiatry*. According to the study, breathing rate quickens and carbon dioxide decreases.[4] Although it is not spelled out, that is an indication of hyperventilation. Similar findings have been published in connection with grief in another study in the same journal which compared breathlessness (dyspnea) in persons with obstructive airway disease and those suffering from depression.

Distinct differences between the way the two groups experienced their breathlessness were noted. In persons with depression, breathlessness occurred when they were at rest, with the main difficulty at inspiration: they experienced a persistent "heaviness" on the sternum, and their breathlessness fluctuated rapidly and was frequently associated with hyperventilation and sighing respiration. Depressive delusions of imminent death were present.

Such symptoms were not experienced in the group of persons with airway obstruction. Their breathlessness occurred on exertion, with the principal difficulty on expiration, and hyperventilation occurred infrequently.

Physical breathing disorders may lead to some of the same symptoms as those experienced by persons with depression and anxiety disorders. When I see persons in my practice who have symptoms of depression and anxiety, I invariably try first to rule out the possibility that these are symptoms of a basic breathing disorder due either to a metabolic or other medical problem such as thyroid deficiency or anemia, or to an obstructive lung disorder such as asthma.

When I see a client for the first time, I always use a spirometer in the initial evaluation.

The "depressive delusion of imminent death" reported here and elsewhere in connection with depression has also been reported as the fear of death in panic attack and in hyperventilation.[5]

Breathing in Anxiety

Anxiety states tend to be accompanied by the following breathing changes:

- Breathing becomes irregular (inspiration/expiration ratio shifts).
- Breathing becomes shallow (tidal volume decreases).
- Breathing rate increases (tachypnea).
- The amount of air flowing in and out of the lungs per minute (minute-volume) increases.
- End-tidal carbon dioxide decreases (hypocapnia).

In short, hyperventilation. Among the few exceptions to these changes are certain psychoses.

Can emotions induce hyperventilation? Looking over all current theories about hyperventilation and depression and anxiety, I am led to the conclusion that, for the most part, persons with the chronic form of hyperventilation are biologically predisposed to these conditions.

The best explanation for how disordered breathing causes psychological disorders is the obvious one: It causes insufficient oxygen delivery to the brain. It starves the brain. The anxiety or depression may stem from the fact that the sufferer is experiencing varying degrees of slow and incomplete asphyxiation—a reduction of oxygen to the body and especially to the brain.

The most likely explanation centers on the effects of low carbon dioxide. We know that when carbon dioxide decreases below normal levels, arteries in the body constrict and brain arteries also constrict. Blood circulation is thus impaired in the brain. That impairment affects the brain's metabolism and therefore its function.

Persons who hyperventilate frequently also report other symptoms associated with impaired brain blood circulation, including dizziness, faintness, disorientation, vertigo, and a feeling of unreality. The symptoms are similar to those experienced when one climbs to an altitude greater than 5,000 feet above sea level.

Low carbon dioxide also causes alkalosis, which makes hemoglobin favor retention of oxygen. Imagine that the hemoglobin molecules are like little magnets. They have to be able to pick up oxygen in the lungs and drop it off in the body tissues. The "magnetism" of the hemoglobin is proportional to the alkalinity of the blood. Within normal limits, a shift toward acidity favors oxygen release.

The red blood cells pick up oxygen in the lungs. But when they get into the tissues, where there is more carbon dioxide due to local metabolism, oxygen is released because the environment in the cells is somewhat less alkaline and the magnetism of the hemoglobin is slightly reduced.

But when carbon dioxide is lost in hyperventilation, and blood shifts to greater alkalinity, oxygen is more tightly bound to the hemoglobin in the red cells, and is not released in normal amounts. This may add to impaired circulation already unfavorable to physical and mental health and well-being.

Low Carbon Dioxide Affects Muscles and Nerves

When blood carbon dioxide levels drop, and there is a slight shift of the blood toward alkalinity, there is an increase in the amount of calcium entering muscles and nerves. Excess calcium in muscles and nerves makes them hyperactive and can cause the spasms called tetany. Muscles will contract more readily, more rapidly, more strongly, and for a greater duration than they normally would with excess calcium.

Chronic low-grade tetany is called spasmophilia and is usually treated with magnesium, which is a natural calcium antagonist. A calcium antagonist protects body tissues from excess calcium.

Although there are exceptions to it, low carbon dioxide generally results in increased nervous system activity. This exaggeration of its typical function is usually attributed to increased nerve cell levels of calcium. It can give you the jitters.

The way that hyperventilation affects the body is poorly understood by most medical practitioners, but were they to understand it, it would be sufficient to explain many of the mental and mood disorders noted in connection with it as effects of low brain oxygen. Every single one of the effects of low carbon dioxide that I am describing to you here is well documented in medical books, and is not controversial.

The DSM-IVR

When a mental health professional must make a diagnosis, it must conform to criteria found in the DSM-IVR, the fourth revision of the *Diagnostic and Statistical Manual of the American Psychiatric Association*. This is the standard reference work for all mental health professionals, and the basis for diagnosis of emotional, character, mood, thought, developmental, psychophysiological, and even substance abuse disorders. Here is another good example of how breathing-related stress, anxiety, and emotional disorders are misunderstood.

There is no reference in the DSM-IVR to hyperventilation. Neither are there index entries for terms commonly relating to breathing difficulties, such as dyspnea or sighing respiration. Yet dyspnea is the first symptom listed under panic disorder:

1. Dyspnea
2. Palpitations
3. Chest pain or discomfort
4. Choking or smothering sensation
5. Dizziness, vertigo, or unsteady feeling
6. Feeling of unreality
7. Paresthesia (tingling in hands and feet)

8. Hot and cold flashes
9. Sweating
10. Faintness
11. Trembling and shaking
12. Fear of dying, going crazy, or doing something uncontrolled during an attack

These twelve symptoms are the diagnostic criteria for panic disorder and none of them is absent from any standard list of hyperventilation symptoms.

Is hyperventilation syndrome synonymous with panic disorder? Clearly, it is possible to have other manifestations of hyperventilation. But in certain persons, the evidence strongly suggests that, for them, it manifests itself as panic disorder, often with agoraphobia.

This brings us back to the notion that psychophysiological disorders are determined by a combination of different factors. The same physical problems may have entirely different expressions in different persons. In one person, hyperventilation may jeopardize oxygen supply to the heart and s/he experiences angina. In another person, there may be artery spasms in the head, with consequent migraine. In yet another person, the symptoms are those of a mental disorder, anxiety and panic attacks, perhaps with phobias including fear of death, or perhaps depression.

Much of the confusion and ambiguity about the role of breathing complaints in physical and mental disorders arises from the diversity of conditions in which it is noted to be present, and from our unreasonable expectation that a given set of complaints is invariably the consequence of the same fixed set of bodily conditions.

You can well imagine that for the physician rigidly trained in differential diagnosis, reason probably dictates that hyperventilation cannot be the cause of all these different conditions.

But what is most important about this is that if you have these "mental" symptoms and you do not feel well, you will not be treated as though you have a medical disorder—you will be told it's all in your mind.

Perfectionism and Breathing Disorders

I have encountered breathing disorders of all kinds in virtually all of my clients. They seem to share certain common features, but they by no means constitute a distinct personality type. They experience anxiety and they appear to overreact—and they are well aware of that fact. That means that they are well aware of the exaggeration of their anxiety reaction to situations that they recognize might leave other persons undisturbed. Their physiological reactions to certain circumstances are just exaggerated.

Some medical researchers have postulated a type of lifestyle component that hyperventilating clients are alleged to have in common. The British pulmonary physician Claude Lum, a pioneer in hyperventilation research, reported that the typical patient showed obsessional and perfectionistic characteristics—a personality type excessively vulnerable to the uncertainties and untidiness of life itself; in other words, an anxious person with a difficulty in coping. No doubt hyperventilators have anxiety in common, and I have seen a number of these other traits, but not sufficiently often to consider them a universal hallmark.

Are Panic Attacks a Symptom of Hyperventilation?

A British research team headed by Dr. D. M. Clark reported that the sensations in panic attacks are similar to those in hyperventilation. The team concluded that, in some persons, stress causes an increase in breathing which results in unpleasant sensations to which these individuals respond with apprehension.[6]

This position is held very firmly by another British expert who titled his report "Hyperventilation as a Cause of Panic Attacks." He contends that panic of sudden onset may represent the physical form of anxiety.[7] This physical predisposition to panic attacks in hyperventilators has been proposed on a number of occasions. People without this predisposition will seldom experience panic attacks in the face of considerable anxiety. What accounts for this predisposition?

One suggestion is an excessive intolerance of the brain to lowered blood carbon dioxide and oxygen, because these gases shift metabolism toward its anaerobic form—a form not preferred by your body—a form in which there are increased levels of lactic acid in the blood.

How would it feel to have this happen to you? Well, breathing would be shallow and rapid and you would feel out of breath, or unable to catch your breath, and, naturally you would wonder why. Your heart might pound in your chest. You might feel numb or even achy.

You would be wondering: Am I having a heart attack? Will my heart suddenly stop? You feel very anxious. Your hands shake and you begin to sweat. Then you would feel strange, perhaps dizzy. Things around you might seem to be unreal. You might experience coldness and numbness, or tingling in your hands and perhaps your toes, and muscle weakness, tremors, and twitches.

You might next figure that you must be losing it, or that you may die. In any event, you are afraid to move about, even perhaps go outside, convinced that the effort will at the very least cause you to pass out. You call your doctor . . . an ambulance. . . . In short, you are experiencing a panic attack.

These are of course the symptoms listed in DSM-IVR in connection with panic disorder, and they are the very same symptoms that are present in hyperventilation.

There are now a number of very provocative research reports that bolster the theory that metabolic changes resulting from hyperventilation lead to panic attacks.

Hypoxia means lack of oxygen, and is usually applied to indicate a severe lack of oxygen. *Graded hypoxia* refers to a less severe lack of oxygen. This designates a sort of chronic reduction in the amount of oxygen delivered to the brain and other body tissues.

Ordinarily, the body's metabolism is about 93 percent aerobic (oxygen combining with glucose to provide energy). In persons with chronic, rapid, shallow breathing, poor ventilation of the lungs will reduce body levels of oxygen. When available oxygen decreases, metabolism changes and there may be an increase, even a doubling, in the proportion of metabolism that is anaerobic. In anaerobic metabolism, the body burns fuels other than glucose. This results in an increase in the body's production of lactic acid, especially in the brain.

An increase in lactic acid cannot be well tolerated by the body, and so it seeks means to restore the acid-base balance. One such method is to increase breathing rate—which, by dumping carbon dioxide from the blood, reduces its acid-forming potential. Most cases of unexplained hyperventilation are now thought to be due to lactic acid accumulation.

If you are a chronic hyperventilator, predisposed to panic attacks, it is simply a matter of time before an acute episode of hyperventilation will be required to clean up body tissues and your blood. Anything that promotes that acute episode will trigger the panic attack as soon as brain levels of lactic acid reach a given level. Panic sufferers have been reported to be more sensitive to brain levels of lactic acid than non-panic sufferers.

Although the reason for the occurrence of panic attacks and agoraphobia is still a matter of debate, there appears to be little doubt that these are breathing related. And it has been my experience that breathing retraining has helped many persons overcome such disorders.

Fear of Flying: Aerophobia

In a complex industrial and geographically decentralized society such as ours, business and professional success frequently depends on the ability to travel. But have you ever noticed feeling inexplicably tired during, or sometimes after, such a trip? Did you yawn and sigh frequently during the flight? Did you suffer headaches? Did you find it difficult to concentrate on a work task? Was it hard to rise out of your seat, to move about the cabin? Were you surprised by sudden unexplained bouts of apprehension and anxiety, or even fear or panic?

Nothing beats traveling by commercial aircraft to get far fast—unless you are among the many hapless persons who fear flying, who suffer aerophobia. Fear of flying, or airplane phobia, is an unusually puzzling phenomenon. What is it the fear of? It is not usually the fear of airplanes, not even of heights. Neither do aerophobic persons particularly fear that they will die in a crash.

The phobia is more like airplane cabin-claustrophobia. What you may fear most is that the cabin door will close, and then you will have the overpowering urge to leave and won't be able to do so. But why should you dread not being able to leave the cabin? Could it be that there is something about the cabin that, perhaps unknowingly, makes you uncomfortable?

Acting on the belief that panic attacks are breathing related, I set about determining what there might be about the aircraft passenger cabin that would affect breathing. Could it perhaps be reduced oxygen in the environment due to the cabin altitude?

The possibility has been largely overlooked that in-flight panic attacks, and a phobic fear of flying, may be related to the way some individuals react to reduced air pressure in the passenger cabin. Because it *is* reduced!

Pressurization assures that the passenger cabin altitude, ranging between 5,000 and 6,500 feet above sea level, differs from the actual aircraft cruising altitude, which may range between 25,000 and 40,000 feet in an average intercontinental passenger jet aircraft. But at 5,000 to 6,500 feet, reduced barometric pressure results in decreased blood oxygen, causing discomfort in most persons who are not adapted to that altitude.

Ordinarily, this reduced level of brain oxygen would be expected to have minimal effects. But in persons who are chronic hyperventilators, or who are otherwise predisposed to breathing-related anxiety and panic disorder, sensations that accompany reduced atmospheric oxygen pressure in the cabin, especially a rapid pulse, may well trigger symptoms. Panic sufferers are very sensitive to chest and heart sensations.

The psychological consequences of low oxygen have been extensively studied by the military. They include impaired judgment, impaired perception, impaired short-term memory, and impaired ability to carry out complex tasks as altitude increases above 4,000 feet. Inappropriate behavior begins to emerge at about 8,000 feet, and finally consciousness is impaired.

On several recent flights, I used a portable oximeter to test the theory that there is a significantly reduced oxygen level in the blood and that this might affect how one feels in an aircraft cabin, perhaps even leading to panic in those so predisposed.

I recorded numerous samples of my blood oxygen level (saturation), pulse rate, and blood pressure, with a probe attached to my right index finger, on two round trips between New York and San Francisco, and one between New York and Reykjavík, Iceland, breathing normally in the (pressurized) aircraft cabin at 5,000 feet and 5,600 feet, respectively, doing deep diaphragmatic breathing at those altitudes. I also took sample readings of the same levels at home, sitting in a comfortable chair, for comparison.

I should add that I was then in my mid fifties, in reasonably good physical condition, and I sometimes (inexplicably) experienced mild apprehension during flight. I certainly had no medical condition that would interfere with blood oxygenation. But I did perform this little experiment mindful of the fact that I have some experience with altitude-related hypoxia in an aircraft with an unpressurized cabin at altitudes reaching to over 13,500 feet.

I discovered that my average arterial blood oxygen level dropped from my typical 96.0 percent to 90.5 percent (norms range between 95.0 and 98.0 percent), and my pulse rate rose from my usual 72.0 to 96.5.

Astonished by a 6.0 percent decrease in blood oxygen—hardly what I'd expected—I tried abdominal breathing by the same method described in the previous section of this book. To my pleasant surprise, my blood oxygen rose to 95.2 percent within three breaths. And I immediately felt the difference, too. But my pulse stayed in the 90s for some time.

Based on my experience, I would recommend to those of you who experience physical and/or psychological effects from reduced aircraft cabin altitude that you consider periodically doing deep diaphragmatic breathing. Take just a few breaths—three or four—so as not to tire your diaphragm.

My little experiment is entirely consistent with the idea that reduced oxygen is associated with apprehension, anxiety, and perhaps phobia and panic attacks. It certainly seems to suggest a reason why one might fear not being able to exit a cabin in which one may experience the symptoms accompanying lack of air.

Bernie: Anxiety and Breathlessness

Bernie is a thirty-year-old divorced insurance executive who devotes a considerable amount of his spare time to physical activity. Although he is shorter than average, he gives the indication of being in good shape. In fact, his dedication to exercise is partly due to his recent realization that he has frequent episodes of breathlessness.

In addition, he reports many of the symptoms associated with hyperventilation: tension and anxiety, occasional dizziness, an unsteady feeling, mild and unexplainable panic attacks, and a moderate chronic depression. His medical complaints consist of low backache, gastritis, low blood sugar, chronic constipation, and coldness of the extremities.

A breathing tracing showed a respiration rate of 16.5 b/min with depressed carbon dioxide averaging 3.8 percent. His breathing showed a predominant chest mode. There was no report of chest pain.

Breathing training was initiated immediately; after a few minutes, he learned deep abdominal breathing. His breathing rate dropped to 4.5 b/min and his carbon dioxide rose to 4.26 percent. Still a little low, but getting there.

Over the next five sessions, he improved markedly and his symptoms began to decrease in frequency and severity. Before he had been instructed to do so, he reported that he had successfully aborted a number of anxiety and panic attacks by using the breathing technique that he had learned. He was, naturally, very pleased with himself for having thought of this on his own.

After the second session, he was referred to my physician colleague for nutritional counseling, and his gastrointestinal and blood sugar problems cleared up as he was getting his anxiety under control.

He remained in training for fourteen sessions, the last ten on a once-every-two-weeks schedule, and training combined with treatment controlled most of his symptoms.

Betty: Cold Hands and Colitis

Betty is a successful twenty-four-year-old artist. Unmarried, she lives alone and travels abroad frequently. She is above average in height and slender. When she first came to see me, she entered my office energetically, and we shook hands briskly. She reported that she experienced tension and moderate anxiety. Her hands were uncommonly cold, and that interfered with her work. Furthermore, she had been under treatment for some time for abdominal problems, including chronic diarrhea, and she seemed to be developing high blood pressure—all anxiety symptoms, she was told.

Her breathing was of the rapid, shallow, high-chest type (21 b/min), punctuated with sighs. Her carbon dioxide was low. She was speeding along. Her blood pressure was elevated at 135/95. And even in a warm room her hands were decidedly cold at 82°F.

Breathing training proceeded rapidly and uneventfully. Within twenty minutes, her breathing rate dropped to 2.75 b/min, her carbon dioxide rose to normal, and her blood pressure dropped to 112/83. Her hand temperature rose to 94°F. Not bad for twenty minutes' work.

Her colitis seemed to me to be somewhat atypical and I suspected lactose sensitivity, food allergy, or folate deficiency. I referred her to my medical colleague. My intuition was correct but my hypotheses were not. The clue was her frequent travels: she had picked up abdominal parasites.

She progressed rapidly and was able, in eight sessions, to warm her hands reliably with abdominal breathing by 8° to 10°F in as little as three minutes.

Frances: Depression

Frances is a thirty-year-old woman, married, with three children. She is a stay-at-home mother. She was referred to me for stress and burnout—an entirely appropriate description of her condition when she appeared in my office. She came in slowly and stoop-shouldered. Her expression was sad and her posture suggested depression and lethargy. Her handshake was limp, her hands cold and sweaty.

She slumped into the chair to which I pointed and she sighed deeply. As she answered my questions, her voice was low, and her tale punctuated by more sighs and chest heaving.

She felt "a wreck," tense, nervous, apprehensive, and anxious. She couldn't catch her breath and felt much of the time as though she were choking. Her husband and children made continuous demands on her for the most menial chores, and refused to lend a hand—even refusing to clean up after themselves. Her husband and one of the children were both verbally and sometimes physically abusive to her.

She experienced abdominal cramps and diarrhea, and was petrified when her heart "skipped a beat." She thought that it was only a matter of time until she had a heart attack and died.

The approach to treatment was multifold.

First, her abdominal distress followed a pattern not uncommon in folic acid deficiency. Second, her severe premenstrual syndrome (PMS) suggested vitamin B_6 deficiency, as well as a nutritional imbalance involving at least her excessive consumption of sweets. In addition, she was tested for anemia and thyroid function. These tests proved negative. She was given a low sugar diet and prescribed vitamins by my physician colleague.

She came to my office once a week to practice deep diaphragmatic breathing with ocean imagery and muscle relaxation. In addition, she was given counseling and assertion training.

Gradually she learned to use breathing to ease her difficulty with self-assertion, and she began to report a lessening of the severity of her symptoms, except on the occasion of an especially bad day. As she began to experience a reduction of her symptoms, and an increased ability to use the breathing to calm herself, it was time for her to return to her primary therapist and resume work on straightening out her dysfunctional family interactions.

Impaired breathing and hyperventilation, or an equivalent atmospheric reduction in available oxygen, may jeopardize the supply of oxygen to the body and the brain, leading to symptoms of anxiety and depression.

The converse of breathe well, be well is that if you're not well, it could be due to the fact that you don't breathe well.

CHAPTER 9

Asthma

Stephanie: Asthma and Breathing Exercises

Asthma is not a psychological symptom. It is a medical disorder. Therefore, when Stephanie left the urgent message with the receptionist at the Institute where I see my clients that she wished me to contact her as soon as possible, I made haste to return her call. When I reached her by phone, she informed me that she was having an exceptionally difficult time breathing that day and that she wished to come to my office, and could I assist her to get her breathing under control?

Stephanie is a twenty-seven-year-old office manager in an import and export firm. She is divorced and has no children. She was referred to me by her physician who thought that breathing training might prove helpful for her. I agreed to do so on the condition that she remain in his care until such time as it was medically justifiable for her to begin to withdraw from the prescription drugs and inhalers she was using.

Stephanie's medical history was not notably eventful, excluding asthma, which she's had since she was a child. But, as is common in persons with asthma, she had the usual plethora of allergies including reactions to foods, various airborne molds, pollens, and dust, and reactions to contact with various materials. She also reported periodic bouts of anxiety.

When I first saw Stephanie, her breathing was typically asthmatic. This means predominantly rapid, uneven, shallow breaths with the exhale relatively brief compared to the inhale. Her exhaled carbon dioxide pattern was all over the place—sometimes up, other times down.

She proved an apt trainee, though, and learned deep diaphragmatic breathing in just four sessions. She was then able to do slow breathing at about three to four breaths per minute with approximately equal inhale and exhale periods and normal end-tidal carbon dioxide concentration. Within about seven to eight sessions, she began to report a lessened need for the inhaler, and its less frequent use.

Asthma is usually defined as a reversible airways obstruction. But for the sufferer, an asthma attack is a frightening inability to breathe, resulting from narrowing of the airways to the lung caused by inflammation, and the resulting swelling and fluid accumulation to which are added spasms of the smooth muscles surrounding the smaller airways, the bronchioles.

Symptoms include wheezing, coughing, and shortness of breath, and are in most cases not life-threatening. But in *intrinsic* asthma (I'll explain later) with irreversible lung changes, life-threatening crises may occur.

A typical asthma attack may begin with an initial phase of hyperventilation. But lung airways restriction may nevertheless impede ventilation enough to cause under- or hypoventilation resulting in decreased blood oxygen. As the attack progresses, some areas of the lungs remain poorly ventilated while other areas try to compensate by hyperventilation.

A detailed study of lung and blood gas concentration in over one hundred asthmatics during acute attacks of bronchospasm was reported in the *New England Journal of Medicine*.[1] Chronic low oxygen was observed in ninety-one of the patients. Seventy-three of them had a condition called respiratory alkalosis, which means that their blood was somewhat more alkaline than it should be. This condition follows carbon dioxide loss by hyperventilation.

When Stephanie came into the office that day, she was wheezy. And as I was preparing her for breathing training, she suddenly experienced an attack. Her breathing rate rose to about 26 b/min and, as is typical, expirations were brief and incomplete. Her exhaled carbon dioxide level sank to 3.6 percent (4.55 percent is normal), and her blood oxygen level dropped to 89.1 percent (95.0 to 98.0 percent is normal).

A noninvasive method is used to measure and monitor blood oxygen concentration. The client's left index finger is inserted into a small infrared sensor device which conducts information about oxygen concentration in the blood flowing through the finger to a medical instrument called an oximeter. This is the same instrument used in a hospital to monitor patients' blood oxygen levels.

Immediately after inhaling albuterol, her breathing remained shallow and erratic, but it slowed slightly to 22 b/min, and her exhaled carbon dioxide level rose somewhat to 3.9 percent. Then her blood oxygen level began to rise sharply to a normal 96.5 percent. After six minutes of rest, she attempted abdominal breathing.

There followed three more breathing training trials, each lasting about three minutes, distributed over a twenty-five minute period. During the last one of these, her breathing rate was about 4 b/min, carbon dioxide normalized at 4.7 percent, and blood oxygen was also in the normal range at 97.5 percent.

Common Types of Asthma

Asthma may take many forms. *Extrinsic immediate atopic asthma* is an immune reaction to common allergens including grass pollens, dust, mold, and animal hair, among others. *Extrinsic late nonatopic allergic asthma* begins at least one hour after exposure to airborne allergens. *Extrinsic irritant and pharmacologic asthma* is precipitated by chemical exposure, sometimes acting directly on the mucosal lining of the bronchioles. The definition applies if removal from the chemical trigger causes resolution of the condition and if reexposure causes worsening.

Intrinsic asthma is thought to be based on a defect in the regulation of the bronchial airways by the autonomic nervous system because no known immunologic abnormalities have been demonstrated in this form. It may be triggered by viral respiratory tract infections, weather changes, exercise, and other factors.

The connection to weather changes should not be surprising since low barometric pressure presents a further problem for gas exchange in an underventilated lung, and positive and negative air ion density has also been related to how the lung exchanges gases.

Intrinsic aspirin-intolerant asthma is associated with ingestion of aspirin, indomethacin, ibuprofen, and tartrazine (FD & C yellow #5 dye), among others. It is associated with chronic sinusitis and nasal polyps. *Intrinsic exercise-induced asthma* is most common in children. However, wheezing and bronchospasm are common after vigorous exercise in many forms of asthma.

Intrinsic infectious asthma is common in children susceptible to recurrent viral upper respiratory tract infections, and *intrinsic asthmatic bronchitis* is characterized by asthma and chronic bronchitis, in which cigarette smoking may or may not be a factor. Cigarette smoking is a factor, however, in intrinsic asthma, with both irreversible and reversible obstructive airways disease.

These forms of asthma include *bronchitic intrinsic asthma*, with reversible airways disease, *emphysematous-intrinsic asthma*, and various combinations of bronchitis, asthma, and emphysema. Both intrinsic and extrinsic asthma are factors in mixed asthma.

As you can see, there are many different forms of asthma, and its diagnosis in any given sufferer is often difficult and sometimes, unfortunately, incorrect.

Psychological Factors in Asthma

There have been many psychological interpretations of asthma, especially in childhood asthma. One psychodynamic theory centers on the concept of conflict and the "muted cry." Others conclude that while actual or anticipated separation or loss is thought to play an important role in initiating attacks in about 50 percent of cases, attacks are also thought to be triggered by many other emotions, both unpleasant and pleasant, as well as by physical exertion. These theories are sufficiently nonspecific to be indistinguishable from theories of stress.

However, it should be pointed out that an anxiety and stress theory of asthma makes little sense because adrenaline, one of the stress hormones that plays a key role in stress, is actually often used to relieve asthma during a severe attack.

Some investigators have found that odors trigger asthma in a remarkably large number of sufferers. This has been ascribed to its psychological properties, but I am more inclined to see it as a connection between asthma and migraine, which is also quite sensitive to odor.

Asthma can be triggered by many of the same things that can trigger migraine, including foods. I therefore encourage my clients to think of asthma as pulmonary migraine, and I make the same recommendations to them in either case: Reduce exposure to known airborne allergens, adopt an *oligoantigenic diet* (see chapter 5), and learn deep diaphragmatic breathing.

Extrinsic bronchial asthma is a reaction of immune system cells to allergens. Only about 40 percent of persons exposed to common allergens develop hypersensitivity to them. Of those who do, less than half develop bronchial asthma. But the formation of antibodies has also been observed to occur in persons who do not suffer asthma. Thus, it may be a necessary but not sufficient predisposing factor.

Medical sources generally hold that immune system cells in the nasal, bronchial, and gastrointestinal lymph tissues first recognize the specific allergens. They then form the specific antibodies. Histamine is then released, causing constriction of bronchial airways and of small blood vessels, increased blood vessel permeability, increased mucous secretion, and increased release of action hormones such as noradrenaline.

Many other important substances are also formed and released, including the slow-reactive-substance-of-anaphylaxis (SRSA), that can cause profound, long-lasting smooth muscle and bronchial muscle contraction. Platelet-activating factor (PAF) may be released by sensitized lung tissue, causing blood platelets to tend to form clumps and to release serotonin, which promotes constriction of bronchial smooth muscle.

Another substance, bradykinin, is produced as part of the reaction and causes bronchoconstriction, low blood pressure (hypotension), increased sweating and salivation, and increased blood vessel permeability. Prostaglandins, especially PGF2, stimulate both bronchoconstrictors and vasoconstriction.

All factors considered, it certainly seems that the lungs release numerous hormones and that their role, ordinarily viewed as more or less passive except for gas exchange, is astonishingly oversimplified. Asthma may be one of the best windows into that complexity.

Nitric Oxide and Asthma

Doctors Maria G. Belvisi, Peter J. Barnes, and colleagues from the Department of Thoracic Medicine of the National Heart and Lung Institute in the United Kingdom recently demonstrated for the first time that the real mechanism which keeps bronchioles in the lungs open is controlled largely by the gas nitric oxide.[2] In 1993, Barnes and Belvisi marveled in the journal *Thorax* that "even five years ago few would have realized that the simple gas nitric oxide (NO) would be involved in the regulation of so many physiological functions."[3]

Their article described the formation of the gas from the amino acid L-arginine by lung lining-cells and macrophages, the forms of the enzymes needed to make it, and its role in blood vessel relaxation and in the dilation of the smaller airways of the lungs called bronchioles. Since then, there has been a considerable advance in our understanding of the nitric oxide connection in asthma.

Another team of researchers from the United Kingdom also showed the production of nitric oxide in the lining of the airways of the lungs. They speculated that it serves to counteract constriction of the bronchioles in asthma. At the same time, researchers from the Karolinska Institute (of Nobel fame) showed increased amounts of nitric oxide in the air exhaled by asthmatics. This finding of increased exhaled nitric oxide in asthmatics was confirmed and explained to be related to the inflammatory process by Dr. Sergei A. Kharitonov and colleagues from the Department of Thoracic Medicine of the National Heart and Lung Institute in the *Lancet* and in the *American Journal of Respiratory and Critical Care Medicine.*[4]

Finally, Dr. Kharitonov, together with colleagues from a pediatrics hospital in Vienna, reported that oral supplementation of the amino acid L-arginine, from which the cells in the respiratory tract make nitric oxide, beneficially raised the level of this gas in exhaled breath.[5]

They compared the effect of three different dosages of L-arginine administered to normal human participants to a placebo control group and found that the higher dosage of L-arginine caused a significant increase in the concentration of nitric oxide in exhaled air. The increase was greatest about two hours after administration. There were no significant changes in heart rate and blood pressure in these patients, and only one of them showed no improvement.

The significance of these findings is underscored by their conclusion that oral L-arginine supplementation increases nitric oxide production in the body and the lungs, and that this may have therapeutic application in diseases where nitric oxide is produced in insufficient quantity, such as asthma. It has also been shown, by the way, that smoking cigarettes lowers nitric oxide production, but that it returns to normal levels one hour after the last cigarette.

Increasing nitric oxide availability in the body by inhaling it has now also been found to have therapeutic effects in other lung and lung-related diseases, including pulmonary hypertension and adult respiratory distress syndrome (ARDS).

Diaphragmatic Breathing Can Reduce the Frequency and Severity of Asthma

The behavioral treatment approach to the reduction of asthma is a three-pronged attack: (1) it aims to reduce known asthma triggers, including those that are airborne and/or food-borne; (2) it focuses the client on undoing dysponetic bracing and other muscle tension with self-awareness and relaxation techniques; and (3) it teaches breathing maneuvers intended to improve breathing efficiency and restore diaphragmatic and thoracic muscle control and degree of muscle contraction (tonus).

On the psychological side, reducing the frequency and severity of asthma attacks has the additional benefit that comes from gaining control, seen in persons with a health or other impairment. To quote a client, "The most meaningful part in the training occurred when I inhaled four thousand milliliters. It gave me the sense of control and hope that I never had before."

Reduction of food triggers, as well as airborne antigens such as pollen or common discarded roach skeleton debris, has been detailed in chapter 5. I will therefore mention here only those items on the list of Dr. Egger and colleagues which had a provocation probability greater than 10 percent:

- cow milk and cow cheese
- citrus fruit
- wheat
- food additives (tartrazine and benzoic acid)
- hen eggs
- tomatoes
- chocolate
- corn
- grapes

The Incentive Inspirometer

Diaphragmatic breathing training can be enhanced by the use of an *incentive inspirometer*. I use the voldyne (Sherwood), a simple unit that can be purchased for about $20 in most drugstores, which permits you to observe inspiratory volume with each training effort. Although the primary problem in most cases of asthma is not inspiratory but expiratory volume, increasing inspiratory volume has a salutary effect on expiration.

Asthma sufferers seem to hold air in reserve. That is, they can readily inhale, but they tend not to exhale quite as fully as most nonasthma clients. By teaching them deep diaphragmatic breathing, especially pulling back the abdomen by contracting the abdominal muscles with each exhale, they improve expiratory volume. Inspiratory volume improves when they exhale more fully. Teaching full inhale also teaches fuller exhale.

The inspirometer is a graduated, transparent cylinder containing a piston. A flexible tubing with a mouthpiece at one end protrudes from the side of the instrument. The trainee can observe maximum inspiratory volume at the end of each breath.

The Inspirometer Training Procedure

The client sits upright facing the inspirometer, which is placed at mouth level, and is instructed to loosen clothing, including the belt and the upper part of the pants zipper, where applicable. Then, s/he is instructed in how to use the voldyne and encouraged by one or two practice trials, to demonstrate that s/he knows how to use it (i.e., in through the mouth, and out through the nose). A small indicator at the side of the instrument rises with inspired volume and can be used to note maximum inspired volume achieved. After each breath, the indicator can be returned to zero.

Baseline recordings are first made with the eyes closed and taking five normal breaths, with time in between to permit the piston to return to zero. These serve as a frame of reference against which one can later gauge the effectiveness of training. The client is then instructed to take five maximum breaths through the voldyne and maximum inspired volume is then recorded each time.

Following this baseline recording, there is an explanation of the benefits of diaphragmatic breathing, including instructions in complete exhalation by contracting the abdominal muscles, thus pulling the stomach in slightly at the end of expiration. The client is then told to inhale slowly, letting the tummy "bubble out" completely, and then to relax the shoulders and chest until the end of expiration.

I usually demonstrate the procedure with my own voldyne unit first. Parenthetically, the trainee is discouraged from any raising or expanding of the chest in breathing.

A similar breathing strategy can also be used with clients with panic and anxiety, because the mastery of effortless breathing adds a sense of control. The training procedure may include teaching the client to relax the shoulders because raising them, or hitching, is quite common in persons who are tense.

Some persons are self-conscious and are therefore reluctant to allow the abdomen to bubble out. This needs to be overcome. Some others may need to practice keeping shoulders relaxed as a primary objective, as opposed to increasing volume. Sometimes it is desirable to have the client demonstrate the problem he or she is having with breathing by exaggerating it so that all its features become clear. Various forms of imagery may be helpful, including "seeing" air swirl into the body with inspiration and swirling out with expiration.

Average breathing training time lasts about fifteen minutes. Five normal diaphragmatic breaths, followed by five maximum-volume diaphragmatic breaths, are recorded after training.

Muscle Tension
Electromyographic (EMG) Biofeedback

Most of the time, breathing training proceeds without the need for monitoring with additional instruments. But in some cases it is desirable to observe muscle activity via (EMG) feedback to control the muscle tension in the neck and upper chest and to help the client to learn not to lift the chest with inspiration.

Electrodes are then applied to the skin surface over the muscles being monitored. Amplifiers transform the tiny electrical current emitted by the muscles as they contract into a visual or auditory signal that changes proportionately with the increase or decrease in the underlying muscle activity.

The regional muscles monitored are the *anterior scalenes*, which arise from the third to sixth cervical vertebrae and attach to the first rib; the *medial scalenes*, which arise from all cervical vertebrae and attach to the first rib, lateral to the anterior scalene; and the *posterior scalenes*, which arise from the fifth and sixth cervical vertebrae and attach to the upper border of the second rib.

The importance of considering the involvement of these muscles in breathing training is that they attach to the spine at the base of the skull and, when they are contracted, they raise the rib cage, an undesirable activity in deep diaphragmatic breathing training.

Considering the anatomical and spatial relationship of the scalene muscles to the right and left trapezius shoulder muscles and pectoral chest muscles, among the many fairly massive muscles of the neck, shoulder, and upper thoracic region, it is unlikely that electrode placement anywhere in the region can be specific to the activity of only the scalenes. But that does not really matter because the concern is with action in that region during chest breathing relative to that in which abdominal (diaphragmatic) breathing prevails. Consequently, I have often adopted the use of the scalene/trapezius EMG mainly as an *error signal* to help the client to learn to avoid chest lifting where it is habitual, and altogether unconscious.

In any event, the task for any client is to learn to breathe diaphragmatically and, most important, effortlessly. One has to learn to reduce upper chest movement, however, to accomplish this.

In the EMG biofeedback procedure, clients are asked to inhale without increasing the sound that indicates the level of EMG activity of the upper thorax. This can only be done if one first exhales sufficiently, by contracting the muscles of the abdominal wall, and then inhales by relaxing the muscles of the abdominal wall, thereby allowing abdominal contents to go down and forward when the diaphragm contracts. The goal of the EMG training is to decrease the activity (EMG) from the upper chest and neck accessory muscles of breathing, while increasing inhalation volume.

There are many different forms of asthma, and U.S. government health agencies warn that their incidence is on the rise. With notable exceptions, many of my clients tell me that they were never told by their physicians that breathing exercises could bring a measure of relief. In every case I have supervised, individuals with severe, even life-threatening asthma were able, after some breathing training, to reduce medication (under their physician's supervision).

Breathing training techniques help persons with asthma to increase otherwise restricted tidal volume and also to overcome the patterns of bracing and other adaptation such as chest lifting that compound the asthma and that, in the long run, further impede proper breathing.

Things to Do

If you suffer from asthma, you may wish to keep in mind that the frequency and severity of asthma attacks can be reduced by certain factors in your environment over which you can exert control.

First, keep in mind that the loathsome invisible dust mites that get into bedding shed bits of discarded skeleton, just like cockroaches wandering about in your home. This material can be inhaled in sleep. Consequently, hypoallergenic pillows and bedding (no feathers or down, please), changed periodically to eliminate their tiny inhabitant debris, can be helpful. In general, maintaining your home in as dust-free a state as possible is essential. Carpeting hinders that effort.

Second, pets such as cats, dogs, and birds are veritable dust mops, as well as hosts to their own universe of microscopic inhabitants, which can cause your pets to itch periodically. Pet turtles have no fur, but they can develop and harbor molds. In very severe asthma, pets can be hazardous to health. Some plants and many flowers have pollens that can trigger attacks.

Third, consider the food lists in chapter 5, and monitor those foods that seem to increase your risk of asthma attack. Do not institute a foods elimination program without medical advice. You could wind up malnourished. It has also been shown that low blood sugar worsens asthma, especially in those who have the exercise-induced form. Controlling your blood sugar level by nutrition and by supplementing dietary chromium with the advice of a physician may also help to avert attacks.

Most forms of asthma are not curable, in the ordinary sense of the word. Medication can help relieve symptoms and so can the self-help steps you take, including doing regular breathing exercises.

CHAPTER 10

Migraine, Epilepsy, and Associated Disorders

The fact is that within a few years every physician who will be expected to be in the race for practice will have to be versed in psychology. He will have to know much concerning the power of thought over organ and functions, and recognize the stupendous fact that within man resides the greatest curative principle, and that it may be directed by the will.
—A. B. Olston, Mind Power and Privileges, 1902

Alice: Migraine

Alice is a seventy-two-year-old widow long retired from secretarial office work. She lives alone. She is average in stature but somewhat overweight. She entered my office briskly and energetically and reported that she wished to learn abdominal breathing because she had heard that it might help her to control her blood pressure and her frequent migraine headaches.

She reported frequent transient moderate depression, arthritis, chronic gastritis, and rheumatic pain, in addition to her elevated blood pressure and headaches. Although her dietary habits were generally good, she reported a craving for sweets, especially sugar.

At the initial evaluation, her breathing rate was found to be 15 breaths per minute (b/min) with low carbon dioxide (3.68 percent). Although a breathing rate of 15 b/min is not notably elevated for a

161

person of her age and physical condition, the carbon dioxide level is much lower than one might expect and arouses suspicion of a low metabolic rate due, perhaps, to a thyroid condition (headaches are a common accompaniment of thyroid conditions).

Her blood pressure was 147/87. She reported that she was prescribed antihypertensive medication but that it "did not agree" with her. During the initial breathing training, she showed remarkably good diaphragm and abdominal muscle control, and training progressed rapidly. At the end of the first training session, her breathing rate was 4.5 b/min and her carbon dioxide rose only slightly, to 3.98 percent. But her blood pressure dropped to 131/77.

She continued periodic training and reported that she had fewer migraine attacks. She also reported that on several occasions she was able to forestall an attack by doing the breathing exercises when she felt the sensations that for her usually preceded migraine.

Are Migraines and Epilepsy Related?

It must seem curious to find migraine and epilepsy lumped together in a chapter in a book about breathing. Are these disorders breathing related?

I'm sure that you've heard that migraine can be brought on by anxiety, tension, and stress. But epilepsy? "Everyone knows" that epilepsy is a brain disorder. Could it possibly be breathing related? Well, it's not caused by bad breathing, but it sure can be triggered by it.

Although medical specialists voice the distinction between migraine and epilepsy with confidence, that confidence may not be based in fact. It is still a matter of conjecture that migraine and epilepsy are entirely different entities. I will make a strong case for the belief that epilepsy is just as much an arterial blood vessel problem affected by breathing as migraine, and that the distinction between epilepsy and migraine boils down, practically, to which arteries are affected—those inside or those outside the skull.

It should be noted that epilepsy-like brain waves are usually produced by overbreathing or "hyperventilation challenge." This means that there is a connection between hyperventilation and abnormal brain waves commonly observed in patients with seizure conditions—another good reason to avoid the procedure, in my opinion.

The use of hyperventilation to elicit abnormal brain wave patterns in routine neurological examination follows logically from the observation that they are invariably produced that way. This was common knowledge to renowned doctors of neurology, such as Hughlings Jackson and Sir William R. Gowers: they discovered before the turn of the twentieth century that a good way of finding out if you had epilepsy was to get you to "overbreathe" and produce a seizure.

As you will see, migraine and epilepsy both respond favorably to breathing training and nutritional management.

The history of migraine goes back several thousand years. Aretaeus (first century C.E.) is said to be the first to have singled it out. It was cited by Galen (129–ca. 199 C.E.), who is credited with the original designation, "hemicrania," which ultimately became "hemigraine," or pain of one side of the head, then "migraine."

A brief history of migraine research must mention Johann Jakob Wepfer, who recognized the relationship between arterial pulsation, arterial dilation, and pain in the early 1700s. Subsequently, the development of a compression test demonstrated that pressure on the carotid artery in the neck, or the temporal artery at the temples, may relieve migraine, and gave impetus to the belief that migraine results from constriction and dilation of arteries.

Sir William R. Gowers, a giant of nineteenth century neurological research, noted many similarities between migraine and seizure disorders, especially in regard to the role of hyperventilation, and he assigned migraine to the "borderland of epilepsy," also the title of his book.

Gowers noted alternation between migraine and epilepsy and recognized "premonitory symptoms," which precede an attack. But he notes that the duration of the attacks is a major distinction between migraine and epilepsy: seizures do not last as long as migraine.

He reports arterial compression by ligature, tying a limb, to be successful in aborting seizures.

Many major historic and literary figures have been alleged to suffer from migraine: Napoléon Bonaparte, Lewis Carroll, Frédéric Chopin, Sigmund Freud, Heinrich Himmler, Thomas Jefferson, Leo Tolstoy, and Virginia Woolf. According to one source, at least one in ten persons in North America suffers migraine in one form or another.

The skulls of prehistoric peoples with trephinations, or burr holes, have been found in Europe and in South America. These burr holes are usually thought to result from religious practices in which evil spirits were alleged to be released. It is to the credit of those who performed this surgery that those skulls show bone healing—the procedure was apparently not intended to be fatal.

If I am permitted speculation, it seems far more likely that these burr holes represent an early attempt to cure headaches, perhaps even migraine. We tend to patronize cultures that we do not regard as being at least as advanced as ours, and attribute all of their rituals to primitive religious practice—usually animistic.

Migraine Symptoms

Migraine is usually understood to mean headache, but in fact it may take different forms, and headache is only one of them. Migraine may involve:

- headache—unilateral or bilateral
- nausea/vomiting
- perceptual disturbances
- auras—disturbed consciousness/dizziness
- sensitivity to light, or scotoma—flashing lights or wavy lines
- smell hallucinations
- auditory hallucinations
- tactual or other hallucinations
- paralysis—usually unilateral
- speech impairment—slurring or aphasia

An excellent description of migraine is given by D. J. Dalessio in his classic book on the disorder.[1] Migraine features periodic headache, usually unilateral in onset but which may become generalized, also irritability and nausea, and often it involves photophobia (avoidance of light), vomiting, constipation, and diarrhea. Not infrequently, the attacks are ushered in by wavy or otherwise distorted visual patterns, scintillating flashes, loss of half the right or left visual field, unilateral sensations in body or limbs, and speech disorder.

The pain is commonly limited to the head, but it may include the face and even the neck. Other bodily accompaniments are abdominal distention, cold bluish extremities, vertigo, tremors, pallor, dryness of the mouth, excessive sweating, and chilliness.

Some persons report feeling exceptionally well the day before an onset, even though changes in their blood vessels may already be apparent then. Sometimes, changes in the nasal mucosal lining, which shows a deep reddening, may be especially noticeable.

The list of symptoms above is not exhaustive, and I am assuming that if you suffer migraine, that diagnosis was made by a knowledgeable physician. Headaches are not invariably caused by migraine. Migraine may also be characterized by symptoms other than headache, such as recurrent nausea and abdominal cramps (abdominal migraine) only.

How can you determine if your abdominal cramps might be migraine? Migraine runs in families: if a parent or sibling has migraine in any form, then your symptoms may be suspected as being migraine as well.

What Causes Migraine?

Rodolpho Low's excellent book *Migraine* teaches us that:

- The onset of migraine occurs before the age of ten years in one-third of all cases.
- Fifty-six percent of migraine sufferers had their first episode by the age of sixteen years.

- The initial episode of migraine occurred before the age of forty years in 90 percent of cases.[2]

Dr. Low's book focuses principally on the role of low blood sugar (hypoglycemia) in migraine. Hypoglycemia is well known to precipitate headache and migraine, and has also often been implicated in promoting hyperventilation.

Most sources agree that the actual cause of migraine is unknown but evidence suggests that it is a vascular event. This means that migraine depends on a disturbance of the arterial blood vessels in the head or abdomen. The event involves first the constriction and then the dilation of the vessels. We also know that serotonin, linked to depression, is involved in the process.

The blood vessel dilation in the painful phase of migraine is commonly treated with ergot derivatives (ergotamine), powerful vasoconstrictors that narrow the arteries, or with newer prescription drugs, such as Imitrex, that inhibit the action of serotonin.

Serotonin is released by the blood platelets when something makes them clump together, or in response to blood vessel injury. That something which makes them clump together, or aggregate, is usually the action of oxygen free radicals, which damages the platelets and can cause them to release a certain platelet aggregating factor.

Anoxia means that there is no oxygen available to body tissue; *hypoxia* means that the supply is curtailed, though not cut off completely. In anoxia, death may follow rapidly. But in hypoxia, depending upon the degree of oxygen reduction, a number of changes in metabolism occur. None of them benefit you.

Many researchers have emphasized the role of low oxygen in migraine. In one article, the author proposes that a brief episode of brain hypoxia occurs in *every* attack of migraine.[3]

But these findings are also consistent with a little-discussed but well-established fact that the brain wave pattern (EEG) in migraine, almost identical to that in many of the epilepsies, has also been strongly associated with hypoxia. It typically shows abnormalities in the low frequency end, or *theta* band of the EEG—between four and seven cycles per second. This is the same pattern as in epilepsy and has led many epilepsy investigators, including the internationally renowned Canadian neurologist Wilder Penfield, to conclude that low blood oxygen (hypoxia) due to reduced blood flow to the brain was responsible for seizures. In fact, the reduced brain blood flow was attributed by Dr. W. Lennox, a noted Harvard neurologist, to the vasoconstrictive effects of low blood carbon dioxide in hyperventilation.

For the most part, the brain wave pattern is directly related to the concentration of carbon dioxide in the blood circulating in the brain, because that concentration correlates with blood flow to the brain. As the carbon dioxide concentration decreases, blood flow to the brain is proportionately reduced. The brain wave frequency then drops from twelve cycles per second (alpha), the relaxation brain wave, to four to seven cycles per second (theta), the seizure brain wave.

I have not seen a single migraine sufferer who did not show hyperventilation and the accompanying brain wave abnormalities. When a combination of breathing retraining and nutritional control reduced the incidence and severity of the migraine attacks, the brain waves always showed the corresponding change toward higher frequency normal patterns.

Such consistently observed low oxygen-related brain wave patterns have been reported in 30 to 40 percent of migraine sufferers by a New York research group. In fact, the high incidence of migraine in epileptic seizure sufferers and the comparably high incidence of seizures in migraine sufferers led one doctor to adopt the use of anticonvulsants in the treatment of migraine in children.

The Migraine-Food Connection

Amines are protein building blocks. They may be manufactured by the body or ingested in food substances. Those that the body cannot manufacture are called *essential amines*, as in vit-*amines*.

Vasopressor amines are those that tend to promote increase in blood pressure. *Vasoactive amines* promote spasm in arteries—alternating their constriction and dilation—as in angina pectoris or migraine. Among these, dopamine, tryptophan, and tyramine play a key role in migraine.

A number of mechanisms are activated by these amines. Principal among these is platelet clumping or aggregation. Tryptophan, commonly found in many foods, including milk, turkey, and avocado, is a serotonin building block. Tryptophan is known to promote drowsiness and sleep. That may be why you feel sleepy after Thanksgiving turkey dinner. Tryptophan may also trigger migraine.

The release of serotonin into the blood is accompanied by the release of histamine. As we have seen, histamine is a vasoconstrictor. Blood flow must be impaired to some degree in the face of constricted arteries and clumping blood platelets. This alone would account for some of the reported low brain oxygen levels.

Release of the platelet aggregating factor in the blood may be precipitated also by tyramine and increased levels of action hormones. That is why your physician may be prescribing beta-blockers to treat your migraine. Beta blockers inhibit the action hormones.

There are several ways in which you may increase blood levels of these amines and the platelet aggregating factor. You can raise your stress level, releasing action hormones. Or you can challenge your blood platelets by loading your bloodstream with tryptophan or tyramine-rich foods.

Bear in mind also that all of these factors are only operative in persons disposed to migraine—which runs in families. As one group of researchers pointed out, it has been shown that the platelets of migraine sufferers release their serotonin content more readily at all times in response to such agents as tyramine than do the platelets of non-migraine sufferers.[4]

Medical research studies have reported a defect in platelet serotonin uptake and accumulation in migraine sufferers, as well as changes in the platelet membrane. Thus, a permanent difference may actually exist in the platelets of migraine sufferers.

Salicylates and Migraine

Some food substances—grapes and whole grains, for instance—are relatively high in salicylates, like those found in aspirin. These foods may interfere in the natural formation of certain protective substances called *prostaglandins*. Most medical researchers are not aware of the concentration of salicylates in foods. For example, a recent report in the *Journal of the American College of Cardiology* attributed to the flavones in grape juice its ability to reduce platelet aggregation more effectively than aspirin.[5] The authors were clearly unaware that grapes, and therefore grape juice, contain one of the highest concentrations of natural salicylates found in foods.

Natural salicylates are also implicated in attention deficit and hyperactivity disorder (ADHD) in children. This was amply shown by Dr. B. F. Feingold, who reported the beneficial effects of removing salicylates from the diets of such children. He suggested excluding all artificial colors and flavorings, all factory-made soft drinks, candies, cakes, puddings, ice cream, luncheon meats, margarine, many processed cheeses, and such foods as:

- grapes
- raisins
- cucumbers
- cherries
- apples
- apricots
- oranges
- nectarines
- peaches
- plums
- prunes
- tomatoes
- strawberries
- raspberries
- anything flavored with natural mint or wintergreen
- any aspirin-containing medication[6]

You may note that this is almost the same list of foods as that given in connection with migraine in chapter 5.

Epilepsy and Hyperventilation

Epileptic seizures are classified by cause or by symptoms. Seizures of readily determinable organic origin, such as brain tumors, lesions, or post-trauma, are said to be *symptomatic*. Those of unknown origin are called *idiopathic*. Seizures may take various forms such as petit mal, grand mal, and psychomotor, varying in frequency and severity. We shall consider here only idiopathic seizures.

Neurology views seizures as the result of brain cell dysfunction reaching a sort of critical mass—brain cells going haywire and producing weird patterns.

Dr. Wilder Penfield, probably the most respected neurosurgeon in the world and an unquestioned authority on epilepsy (having pioneered its surgical treatment) wrote that hyperventilation elicits changes in the EEG and seizures in epileptic patients by causing a partial reduction in brain blood circulation due to the brain blood vessel constriction that accompanies the lowered carbon dioxide concentration.[7]

If hyperventilation reduces blood levels of carbon dioxide, causing brain arteries to constrict and limiting oxygen availability to brain cells, no wonder they rebel. Dr. Penfield actually observed arteries constricting just before a seizure, during spontaneously occurring hyperventilation in a patient on whom he was operating. But two scientists, Doctors Darrow and Graf, observed it earlier in mechanically hyperventilated cats.[8] They must have been astonished by the appearance of the constricting brain blood vessels because they referred to them as having the appearance of "sausage links." This is an uncommonly graphic description. Penfield referred to "blanching" as the blood drained from the area served by the pulsating constricting artery.

Why do some persons get seizures and others do not? Why does migraine seem to occur more frequently in persons with seizures, but seizures not as frequently in persons who suffer migraine?

If there is predisposition, what is predisposed? And, if breathing is involved, why do some persons have the tendency to suffer breathing-related seizures while others do not? What can we learn from another blood vessel disorder said to be related to migraine and epilepsy, such as Raynaud's disease (discussed below)?

I maintain that contrary to popular opinion, epilepsies are not the result of disease of the nervous system. "What?" you say. "Seizures are not due to the massive discharge of neurons in the brain?" Right. They are not *due* to it. I have some really convincing evidence to support this otherwise maverick statement.

While director of the Rehabilitation Research Institute at the International Center for the Disabled, I conducted research aimed at developing behavioral methods of epileptic seizure control. Some promise had been shown by methods developed by Doctors M. B. Sterman, in California, and J. Lubar, in Tennessee, through "conditioned" brain waves. After reviewing some four thousand medical research articles and books on epilepsy, I agreed with a minority of epileptologists that seizures are due to arterial blood vessel spasms, just like migraine. The brain electrical discharge observed in seizures, it seemed to me, was the *result* of the seizure, not its cause.

I confirmed, as did many others before me, that hyperventilation preceded each seizure, and I devised a method for biofeedback-assisted breathing retraining to reduce the frequency and severity of seizures in persons whose condition did not respond satisfactorily to anticonvulsant medication.

The results of this work were published in the journal *Psychosomatic Medicine.*[9] Several other publications on the same topic followed.

Raynaud's Disease and Breathing

Are you one of those persons who always has cold hands and feet? One of those who seem to suffer more than most when the weather turns cold? The coldness and spasms in fingers and toes, first described by Dr. Raynaud in 1862, was thought by him to be due to "anxiety neurosis."

The *Lancet* featured an article that mentions the challenge of the "anxiety neurosis" assumption and attributed the spasms to "local fault," meaning some anatomical weakness.[10] Others have reported abnormality in the anatomy of the capillaries in Raynaud's sufferers in the *Journal of Laboratory and Clinical Medicine*.[11] A Tufts Medical College study reported finding abnormal capillaries in the fingernail fold in patients with "neurosis," epilepsy, and migraine.[12]

In the Tufts report, 88 percent of chronic anxiety patients showed the same capillary abnormality as those with the epilepsy and/or migraine. But only 4 percent of those who merely had anxiety did so. The abnormal capillary picture was the same in persons with epilepsy or migraine.

If these studies accurately depict abnormal capillaries that restrict blood flow to various parts of the body in persons with Raynaud's disease, migraine, or seizures, that would certainly qualify as "predisposing."

Breath Power

A. B. Olston writes that he has

> a friend who can, by attention, rush the blood to his feet and warm them when they are cold. This is simply a matter of training. The subjective mind has power to deflate the arteries to any part, or to contract them. The success of such efforts depends simply upon the obedience of the subjective mind. That obedience to subjective instruction is acquired by training.[13]

No behavioral scientist today would find that statement particularly surprising, but it must have been sensational, perhaps smacking of the supernatural, in 1902.

In fact, it is this ability—self-hypnosis—that led Doctors J. H. Schultz and W. Luthe to develop *autogenic training*, a set of postures and relaxation exercises aimed at reducing muscle tension and developing control over anxiety and excessive arousal. It should not surprise you to hear that most people spontaneously notice a decrease in breathing depth and rate when doing these exercises.

Nor would Olston's report be astonishing to the many thousands of persons who have done hand warming by biofeedback as part of the treatment of migraine and Raynaud's disease or Raynaud's syndrome. In other words, the self-regulation of blood flow through the extremities has been shown to be a readily learnable task.

We're talking about arteries and blood flow here, and delivering oxygen to the brain and other body tissues. Hand warming is supposed to tell us that blood circulates better through the hand. So the hand becomes a way of gauging what's going on in the body, also the brain.

How do you learn hand warming? Each clinician has a preferred routine. Biofeedback, for instance, boils down to trial and error. A temperature sensor is taped to the fingertip—the right index finger, let us say. It is connected to an electronic device with a readout display—some of these are like meters, others are digital—showing numbers. The whole thing acts as a very sensitive thermometer.

By trial and error, you can learn to increase fingertip temperature, getting feedback from the readout display. But savvy clinicians may teach their clients various relaxation methods, which are then included in the trial-and-error activity.

In Raynaud's, dilating arteries makes sense, since Raynaud's appears to be the result of blood vessel constriction on top of "local fault." In the case of migraine and seizures, we also assume artery and capillary narrowing is impeding blood circulation to brain cells.

But the first thing that struck me when I was trying brain wave conditioning to control epilepsy was the connection between conditioning and breathing.

A California researcher, Dr. M. B. Sterman, reported the reduction of seizures by the enhancement of a particular brain wave, which he named the *sensory motor rhythm*. Further work on cats resulted in the observation that this rhythm was observed when the cats seemed to be regulating their pattern of respiration during brain wave conditioning.[14]

I thought that curious—reducing seizure activity in the brain occurs in the presence of a brain wave associated with regulation of breathing. Well, hadn't all that previous research also shown that deregulation of the brain followed hyperventilation, which is a deregulation of breathing? And could it be that the brain wave being observed in these more recent conditioning studies was simply that which accompanied regulated breathing—which, of course, reduces seizure activity?

Right or wrong, this reasoning led me to look at breathing during that type of conditioning. It came as no surprise to me that the seizure-reducing brain wave occurred when there was a notable decrease in the blood level of carbon dioxide. Just as had been shown many times in the past.

Continuing along this line of reasoning, I then decided to focus on teaching my patients abdominal breathing, which normalizes blood levels of carbon dioxide. It worked quite nicely. Normal levels of carbon dioxide restored by the breathing method I had developed were also going to other parts of the body, not just the brain. And since normalizing carbon dioxide in circulating blood results in dilation and restoration of blood flow, there should be a change in fingertip temperature corresponding to a decrease in the brain wave seizure pattern. Guess what? It worked in as little as three or four breaths.

I wrote this book, in part, to tell you that deep abdominal/diaphragmatic breathing improves body oxygenation and that this helps you to relax and increase your fingertip temperature, a good thing to do if you have a stress-related or anxiety disorder, or migraine, Raynaud's, or epilepsy. *You can control your blood circulation faster and more reliably by learning deep abdominal (diaphragmatic) breathing than by any form of biofeedback!*

Terry: Cold Hands and Seizures

Terry is a thirty-five-year-old New York City social science teacher. She is unmarried, but has been in a long-term exclusive relationship with the man with whom she is presently living. She is of average height, but slightly overweight. And she reports herself to be in very poor physical and emotional shape. During the initial interview, her handshake was limp and her hands ice cold. She was stooped and gave the impression that she was depressed and that walking itself was an enormous effort. She spoke softly.

As her story unfolded, she stopped several times and sighed deeply. On two occasions, she burst into tears spontaneously. She reported feeling depressed, anxious, and suffering from chronic tiredness and relatively frequent panic attacks. She expressed hopelessness.

Her physical symptoms included migraine, whole-body pain, temporomandibular (jaw) joint pain (TMJ), bouts of mononucleosis (Epstein-Barr), frequent hives, frequent thirst, documented hypoglycemia, hay fever and other allergies, muscle spasms, vertigo, periodic involuntary anorexia and weight loss, and episodes of inability to swallow food or water. She also indicated that she had petit mal seizures.

During the initial interview, she seemed very anxious. Her hand temperature was 78°F in a room at 77°F—1° above room temperature, in a warm room! Her breathing rate was 15 b/min with deep chest breaths, and her carbon dioxide was elevated to 5.9 percent, suggesting hypoventilation, the opposite of hyperventilation, possibly due to an allergic asthma-like lung condition.

Because of the allover pain, I first suspected a thyroid condition, but because she reported having petit mal seizures, I thought it equally possible that she was having seizures equivalent to the temporal lobe type (TLE). Severe and unyielding depression—even suicidal impulses—and panic attacks are well documented in temporal lobe epilepsy. And if the latter were the case, quite possibly the pain is hallucinated.

Her brain wave pattern (EEG) showed diffuse epileptiform waves on both sides with more on the left side.

A breathing maneuver was employed to see whether she had good control of her diaphragm and if her hand temperature would improve and her EEG would normalize. Then she was taught abdominal breathing. The breathing tracing showed a peculiar kind of expiratory spasm on exhale.

Up to that point, I had never seen anything quite like this and I was at a loss to explain it to her. It seemed almost like small spasms of the diaphragm, or chest muscles—a sawtooth expiration pattern. I have since learned that this breathing pattern is called *cardiac oscillation* and that it comes about during expiration when the abdomen pushes the lungs back against the heart. It is, in fact, a good indication of very deep breathing. I was not surprised to learn that this pattern was previously said to be "diaphragmatic flutter," and was once thought to be a manifestation of "hysteria."

Terry showed some apprehension about relaxing, but by the second session she breathed abdominally in training at 3 b/min, with carbon dioxide at 4.76 percent. Quite normal. With continued breathing training, her brain waves showed normalization, although there was still some minimal abnormal activity on the right side.

She continued breathing training for several more sessions and derived a measurable degree of relief from it. But her many underlying medical conditions required more aggressive intervention and she was placed in the care of a physician.

Although they are entirely different clinical entities, migraine, Raynaud's disease, and epilepsy appear to share certain common characteristics. They appear to run in families, and to be related to the reaction of the body and brain blood vessels to low tissue oxygen.

Migraine, Raynaud's, and epilepsy appear to be dependent on possibly inherited anatomical predispositions. But other factors may lower the threshold to attacks, including the apparently additive effects of low blood carbon dioxide and oxygen that follow hyperventilation, and of foodstuffs that can cut blood flow to brain and body tissues. These conditions can respond well to behavioral strategies that include diaphragmatic breathing training.

PART FOUR

Music, Breathing, and Relaxation

CHAPTER 11

Music and Breath: A Sound Connection

One of the most challenging tasks in breathing retraining is to get people to exhale fully. Asthmatics, for instance, give the impression of holding some air in reserve in anticipation of future need. And people who hyperventilate do not seem to have the ability to contract the diaphragm fully. It therefore becomes a continuous struggle to get the proper exhalation so that the next breath will be fuller.

In order to improve breathing, I have often adopted a combination of instructions for imagery, and I have recently added music to the training procedure, with notable results. Although many therapists report using music as an adjunct to relaxation, the conventional wisdom teaches us little about its actual effects on us.

There are numerous references to the bodily effects of music in alternative publications. Numerous studies report that various forms of music relieve tension, anxiety, and pain, and lower muscle tension, pulse rate, and blood pressure while they increase endorphin release.

The less conventional scientific publications report the use of music in helping the mother-to-be to relax during birthing, and to reduce the experience of pain in all sorts of chronic cases, especially intractable cancer. Pioneering this work is a group at the Kaiser Permanente facility in California.

Among the pieces most widely cited in that context are the New

Age compositions of Steven Halpern, including the well-known *Anti-Frantic Alternative*, *Crystal Suite*, and *Crystal Cave;* Sound Rx, which has been used widely as relaxation music; Kitaro's *Silk Road;* Canyon Records; and the various "Environments," including *Slow Ocean*, Syntonic Research, Inc.

These are all fine music pieces, and there are comparable others. But there is nothing about them that helps us to understand how they relax us.

The Growth of Meditation

The 1960s saw the birth in the United States of a popular youth movement that focused its attention on "mind-expanding" hallucinogenic drugs. This involvement with the "inner experience" kindled interest in meditation and music because these affect consciousness. It also came to the attention of science.

Fueled by studies of the relationship between meditative states of consciousness and brain waves in the yogic meditative state,[1] subsequent research also showed the benefits of meditation in reducing muscle tension and elevated blood pressure. Other benefits included deeper, slower, and rhythmic breathing; slower pulse rate; and brain wave patterns predominating in the relaxation-related alpha waves.

It was also noted that this state of meditative relaxation feels good, but more startling was the discovery that its long-term effects were beneficial for persons who suffer from anxiety and stress-related disorders—especially hypertension and cardiovascular diseases.

For some devotees, the initial interest in meditation was fueled by the spiritual wish to transcend common daily life, while for others it was an avenue to reduced anxiety, reduced muscle tension, and lower blood pressure. But the trend to meditation soon took on the characteristics of a fad, and various gurus emerged to lead meditation cults. The cultists eventually dwindled as other, newer cults emerged to take the place of meditation.

Nevertheless, the scientific meditation studies made a popular impact by showing that we can control our brain waves and slow our heart; their legacy is the relaxation techniques currently being used by clinicians. There are several forms, including Herbert Benson's *relaxation response*, one of the better known.[2]

These techniques are, for the most part, combinations of various elements of the original transcendental meditation (TM), or Zazen, methods, which have been abbreviated to reduce the amount of time required to practice them. Their universal aim is to divert the practitioner from the cares of the day by focusing on breathing, muscle relaxation, and pleasant mental imagery. In many instances, this occurs against a background of music—especially New Age music.

How Does Music Affect the Way We Behave?

There are reports of other studies of the mental and physical effects of music in scientific publications. Various forms of music relieve tension, anxiety, and pain. But we know relatively little about *how* we perceive music and *how* it affects us.

In an interesting address to the Music Research Foundation Symposium, at the New York Academy of Sciences, I. A. Taylor and F. Paperte stated that "music cannot be separated from perceptual, symbolic, and personal processes—particularly emotional and physiologic—if one is to understand how music induces and modifies human behavior."

The authors also provide other insights. First, emotions evoked by music reside in the individual, not in the music. Second, music, because of its abstract nature, may bypass intellectual control and directly contact lower centers of the brain. Curiously, covert movement and simple motor activities such as tapping in accompaniment to music have been reported to improve mental ability.

Third, though music may act indirectly on emotions by arousing associations and images in the intellect, its structure (rhythm and tempo) may evoke covert as well as overt movements, which also give expression to emotion. This expression may be without symbolic or latent content and is, therefore, joyful and nonthreatening. But the most significant finding in their report is that the main effect of music is principally either stimulation or relaxation.[3]

A number of recent books detail the effects of music, including Don Campbell's *The Mozart Effect*.[4] Steven Halpern, in *SoundHealth*, reports that music may have a paradoxical effect.[5] Subjective reports of persons listening to Liszt's Liebestraum no. 31 reported it to be "highly relaxing, soothing and meditative," even though their physiological reactions to the music showed otherwise.

Three conclusions can be drawn from Halpern's findings. First, externally imposed rhythm is rarely as relaxing as the personal internal rhythm. Relaxation will happen at the psychological and physiological level when the body can express its own inner nature and harmony.

Second, relaxation may vary in depth. Some types of classical music can produce light relaxation, which may show none of the physiological characteristics of deep relaxation. Most people can't tell one from the other, but their long-term effects may be different.

Third, neutral compositions found predominantly among classical and New Age compositions—those that do not bring forth images—appear to allow the body and mind to move into a mental pattern where the listener seems able to visualize a personal therapeutic imagery and utilize mental self-healing capacities.

In *The Healing Energies of Music*, H. A. Lingerman cites specific examples of what music can do. It can:

- increase physical vitality
- relieve fatigue and inertia
- pierce through moods, uplift feelings
- calm anxiety and tensions
- focus thinking, clarify goals
- release courage and follow-through
- deepen relationships and enrich friendships
- stimulate creativity and sensitivity
- strengthen character and constructive behavior
- expand consciousness of God and horizons of spirituality[6]

Different instruments seem to affect different aspects of the self. The aspects affected are:

- physical body: brass, percussion, electronic music
- emotions: woodwind, strings
- mental: strings
- soul: harp, organ, wind chimes, high strings

Music for the body includes:

- Elgar, "Pomp and Circumstance"
- Schubert, "Marche Militaire"
- Copland, *Rodeo*

Music for feelings and moods includes:

- Brahms, Piano Concerto no. 1
- Handel, Harp Concerto
- Pachelbel, Canon in D
- Bruch, "Scottish Fantasy"

Music for clear thinking includes:

- J. S. Bach, Brandenburg Concertos
- Baroque string music of Telemann, Vivaldi, Albinoni, Corelli, and others.

Music for meals and good digestion includes:

- Vivaldi, lute concertos
- Mendelssohn, string trios
- Mozart, Concerto for Flute and Harp

Music to help you sleep includes:

- Barber, Adagio for Strings
- Debussy, "Clair de Lune"

In *The Healing Forces of Music*, however, Dr. Randall McClellan avers that there is currently no scientific explanation for why we respond to music in the first place. While the auditory nerve stimulates a brain center thought to be the seat of emotion, which also stimulates the frontal cortex responsible for the intellectual interpretation of the sounds, it also sends impulses to another brain region triggering the so-called thalamic reflex, which is noted as rhythmic foot-tapping, swaying, and nodding the head. The thalamus also influences metabolism and controls waking/sleeping cycles, hormone release, pulse rate, and blood circulation.[7]

McClellan cites the work of Helen Bonny, a noted music therapist, which centers on recognizing the value of music in helping the listener to enhance, prolong, and experience his or her personal mood on a deeper level. Bonny selected a wide variety of compositions, mostly from Western classical tradition, and catalogued the selections according to their compatibility to eight mood groups:

1. Solemn
2. Tragic
3. Tender
4. Tranquil
5. Humorous
6. Joyous
7. Dramatic
8. Majestic

Thus, music may serve to help one:

- explore one's inner self
- develop self-awareness
- clarify personal values
- release blocked-up psychic energy
- enrich group spirit
- bring about deep relaxation
- foster religious experience[8]

How Music Moves the Spirit and Breath

There are two types of spiritual music. One type leads to a trance state, the other type leads to the meditative state. Trance most commonly results from repetitive rhythmic patterns sounded simultaneously over long periods of time. Trance is utilized by societies in which shamanistic rituals dominate spiritual experience. Drums typically play a significant role in the procedure.

Music for meditation, on the other hand, affects the mind first and the body second. It creates an atmosphere conducive to stillness and inner contemplation. It is quieter and slower; a melodic phrase may last as long as the inspiration phase of breathing. Its purpose is to slow and deepen breathing, altering perception of time by focusing us on the present moment.

Contemporary American meditative music is derived chiefly from Eastern music, especially that from India as popularized by Ravi Shankar. It is the most common basis for relaxation-therapy adjunct music presently used in the United States. It possesses some of the following characteristics:

- Melody: Older types used only three tones; newer type uses up to seven diatonic tones, and melody progresses by steps with few "skips"
- Duration of phase: Equal to one breath
- Loudness: Moderate to soft
- Rhythm: Smooth and flowing with no sudden rhythmic changes
- Tempo: Slow to moderate pitch change
- Silence: Periods of silence equal to one breath
- Tonal quality: Flutes, strings, and voice
- Texture: Simple (Western music is frequently too complex, and arouses emotions)
- Emotional content: Not intended to express personal emotional content; emphasis on transpersonal peacefulness and inner joyousness

The meanings, associations, and emotions experienced in music are shared by members of a culture. Others may learn to appreciate it, but they will not likely share associations with it. But there is reason to assume that there may be some elements in both Eastern and Western classical music traditions that transcend tradition: characteristics of certain Western music create a dynamic energy in which a sense of pressing forward leads to anticipation, sweeping us along to the inevitable resolution and release.

McClellan proposes a number of pan-cultural healing characteristics of music. Here are some of them:

- Pulse: At or below heart rate (72 beats per minute) for calming and reducing tension. Slightly above heart rate (72–92 beats per minute) for energizing. Triple meters slow breath more effectively than double meters.
- Rhythm: Smooth and flowing at all times for integrating internal body rhythm with energy flow.
- Drones: Without pauses, have meditational and calming effect.
- Pauses: When at slow pulse rates, harmonize and integrate internal body rhythms, and breath and heart rate. At fast rates, can lead to a frenetic state. Pauses can produce a trance in the listener.
- Melodies: Slow and sustained for meditational purposes; pitch sequences primarily by step; at heart pulse rate or slightly faster for energizing purposes; tones drawn from the modes of five, six, and seven tones, predominantly diatonic and asymmetrical. Avoid too many cadences.
- Dynamics: Very soft to moderately loud, depending on the composer's intent; no violent contrasts of loud and soft; change in dynamic levels should be slow and gradual, never sudden.
- Harmony: Used sparingly, if at all. When used, harmony should be modal and diatonic; harmony should be restricted to triads; avoid sevenths and ninths as they are too thick; movement of chord changes should be extremely slow.
- Duration: Minimum of fifteen minutes of steady music; twenty to forty-five minutes optimum duration.

- Texture: Drone plus maximum of two voices for calming purposes. Voices should be widely spaced from each other.
- Tone quality: Generally the softer quality instruments; most common ensemble—flute, strings, and voice; others—pure organ tones (no vibrato), synthesizer when made to sound like organs, or other acoustic string and wind instruments.
- Resonance: Time should be sustained from four to eight seconds using either natural or electronic reverberation for calming purposes. Minimum reverberation for faster tempos when intention is to energize.
- Phase structure: Smooth and flowing; one phase should last for the duration of one slow expiration of the breath as a minimum length when the intention is to calm.[9]

Other pan-cultural characteristics of music are the physiological and brain changes that some selections can be shown to produce.

According to one authority, Dr. D. Schuster, a professor of psychology at Iowa State University, listening to music while studying is also very calming.[10] And, Dr. O. Caskey, a psychologist with the El Paso (Texas) School District, says that "reviewing material while listening to baroque music—music that has approximately one beat per second, such as Bach, Handel, Vivaldi—helps keep you in a relaxed state of mind."[11]

Speaking about his own musical compositions—some of them to the baroque beat, and designed as counter-stress measures—Dr. Steven Halpern writes that "music brings you to a balanced brain state so that you're able to absorb, retain and recall information more easily. . . . It improves your creativity."[12]

I rather favor the slower movement of some baroque works to relax and enhance learning, including the Pachelbel Canon in D, the Mozart Piano Concerto no. 21, and the Albinoni Adagio in G.

How Music Affects the Nervous System

That music has a calming or exciting influence on the hearer is common everyday experience. . . . (But) do we realize that we enjoy music not so much for what it is but for what it does? The accelerated breathing rate, the increased blood pressure, the heightened bodily tonicity, the feeling of power and the reserve of strength make us supermen as we react to music. Blood composition, blood chemistry, blood distribution, blood pressure are all influenced by music. Equally important and extensive respiratory changes also take place under musical stimulation. Without these physiological reverberations music would be quite ineffectual, physically and mentally."

So says Professor J. Kwalwasser of Syracuse University in his book *Exploring the Musical Mind*.[13] But the autonomic nervous system reaction to music is not so simple as that described above, according to G. Harrer and H. Harrer in *Music and the Brain*. Employing the most modern and up-to-date recording equipment, they studied the nature and extent of these bodily changes and reported the following:[14]

- The automatic/physiological (autonomic) response to music depends on (1) individual constitutional factors such as age, gender, lifestyle, physical fitness, health, and temporary states of arousal such as those induced by coffee; (2) prevailing emotional factors; (3) attitudes toward music and its role in one's life; and (4) attitude toward the musical selection.
- The physiological system most affected by music depends on (1) individual patterns, so that in some persons respiratory changes predominate, while in others it is cardiovascular; and (2) the type of music, such that dance music and marches tend to result in motor responses, while others may induce respiratory or cardiovascular changes.
- There are significant differences between the listener and the performer.
- Studies of Herbert von Karajan, while he was conducting Beethoven's Leonore Overture no. 3, showed that his highest pulse rate did not occur at the point of maximum physical effort, but during those passages with the greatest emotional impact for him—those he later singled out as being the most profoundly touching. At these moments, his pulse rate doubled.

When it is stimulated by music, the autonomic nervous system can cause the following changes: cardiovascular arousal can be observed as pulse rate increases in response to music. In short selections, a decrease below resting baseline is seldom detected. An increase in pulse rate may be just as likely to be an expression of pleasure or disapproval. Pulse patterns are fairly consistent when the same piece of music is repeatedly played to the same person.

It is sometimes possible to "drive" pulse rate (increase or decrease) by dynamic changes in music volume or change in rhythm. Relaxing and pleasure-charged passages, and sometimes the ending of a piece, may give rise to changes in pulse rate synchronously with respiration rhythm.

Both arterial blood vessel constriction impairing blood circulation and dilation promoting it have also been observed in response to music, indicating that the response is not specific.

Autonomic nervous system arousal also causes changes in respiration: changes in frequency and depth of respiration occur with concomitant changes in the relationship between inhale and exhale—toward rhythmic or arrhythmic.

However, individual response to music is highly stable and reproducible with repetition of the same piece of music. Intra-individual consistency corresponds to the attitude toward the musical piece. In conventional Western/classical music, intra-individual differences are less significant than for other types of music.

In musical selections with prominent accelerations or decelerations of rhythm, there is a tendency to primary pulse synchronization in some persons, while others show synchronization of breathing rhythm. This suggests that it is possible to differentiate persons as primarily "circulatory" or primarily "respiratory" reactors.

Stimulation by music also results in changes in muscle tension throughout the body. Depending on the type of music, there may be differentially increased muscle activity. Muscle action potentials increase sharply in the legs but only slightly in the forehead. A reverse effect is found when doing mental arithmetic tasks: muscles of the forehead (frontalis) tighten, while muscles in the legs relax.

In a study of persons listening to Bach's Brandenburg Concerto no. 1, pulse rate was found to increase at the beginning and continued at a raised level. At the end of the selection, pulse rate oscillations occurred synchronously with respiration, indicating an alteration in respiratory regulation. Respiration accelerated at the beginning, coupled with decreased breathing (tidal) volume, which increased again later on in the performance. At the end of the piece, respiration dropped to half of peak rate. Results were reproduced with repetition of the performance.

Increased muscle activity, pulse, and respiration that occur in response to the musical selection are expressions of a generally raised level of activation. But this activation is qualitatively different from the activation associated with stress: it involves muscle groups opposite to those active during mental tasks.

Music, Strength, and Endorphins

When a person is asked to squeeze an ergometer, a device used to measure the strength of a hand grasp, while listening to music, the strength of the grasp is invariably reduced significantly. This is further indication that the activation of motor responses, pulse rate, and respiration reflects a qualitative change in the pattern of responses.

What we learn from this is that listening to music may be similar in its effects to doing mild exercise to relieve tension. Exercise is physically activating and may even be strenuous, yet its overall effect is to relax and reduce physical and mental tension. But there are yet other aspects of musical experience that contribute to its salutary effects.

It has been hypothesized that another physiological effect of music is the increased release of endorphins in the brain. Endorphins are the brain's own natural form of morphine—the "feel good" medicine—produced by meditation and running. Its release into the bloodstream is reported to produce a dreamy and extremely pleasurable sensation.

Your Left and Right Brain

No discussion of the effects of music is complete without an examination of right-brain function. According to many neurophysiologists, the right (brain) hemisphere is generally regarded as playing only a minor role in most persons. Since we are principally verbal beings, and language is a predominantly left hemisphere function, we tend to emphasize left hemisphere activities, especially those revolving around speech communications.

In clinical and scientific studies involving persons whose left hemisphere has suffered damage, it has become clear that while speech is impaired, musical ability is not. These studies have given a new perspective to the function of the right hemisphere.

In the evolution of the human brain from that in creatures believed to be little differentiated from their ape ancestors, the gradually increasing requirement for communication and information processing and storage contributed to gradual hemisphere specialization—the analytic and sequential functions of language on the dominant left hemisphere (in 97 percent of the population), and synthetic, spatial integration, and holistic relations on the right.

Nonhuman animals, no matter how complex their communication, do not show hemisphere specialization. The left hemisphere specialization is a function of the complexity of the human world. It is precisely that complexity that is said to lead to the mental and physical stress that is injurious in the long run.

Although the perception of music appears to involve sequences, a left hemisphere function, the evidence points to holistic recognition—like an image that is recognized as a whole rather than as a composite of its parts. And imagery is an important relaxation strategy.

The evolution of Western music may be thought to point to a gradual shift of the focus of music processing by the brain—from the minor hemisphere in baroque or classical music to the major hemisphere in today's avant-garde music.

When stimulated by music, the right hemisphere of the brain

becomes more active, relative to the left side. This is precisely what has been reported to happen in yogic meditation studies with the attendant altered state of consciousness. It is also what happens in deep diaphragmatic breathing.

Stimulated means that blood flow increases to that area, resulting in increased metabolism. By increasing the stimulation to a given portion of the brain, neurophysiologists tell us, we increase its function, or role. Increased blood flow and metabolism in specific areas of the brain are always related to increased activity in those areas. Increased right hemisphere blood flow and metabolism are invariably observed in the deep meditative state that has proven so beneficial in relaxation and in hypertension treatment. Stimulating the right side of the brain is, in the words of Dr. Steven Halpern, an "anti-frantic" strategy.[15]

The right/left hemisphere synchronization, which I have personally observed many times in my clients during deep relaxation, indicates a reduction of the dominance of the left side—the one involved in language and anxiety.

I have used music extensively in teaching abdominal breathing in connection with the treatment of stress-related and psychophysiological disorders, and I will try to translate that experience into a format you can use and enjoy.

How to Breathe with Music: Exercises

Once again, you will have to read through the instructions and memorize them so that you can apply them in a relaxed state, with your eyes closed, while listening to music. The pieces that I like best are Daniel Kobialka's *Timeless Motion* and *Path of Joy*, especially "Pachelbel Kanon," and "Jesu, Joy of Man's Desiring." I use these music pieces to accompany abdominal breathing. With alert healing, or alert energy, I like to use Jean Michel Jarre's *Oxygène*.

With beach imagery, I use two tape recorders and softly, barely audibly, superimpose ocean waves on one of the Kobialka pieces.

Let's try it. Here is what you might do:

Let's assume that you have been doing the exercises and that you now can sustain deep abdominal breathing without effort, and without getting dizzy, for at least five to ten breaths.

Please sit back in your comfortable chair or recliner, loosening your collar and belt, and so on. Close your eyes and focus your attention on your nostrils. Try this for three breaths.

Did you feel how cool and dry and refreshing your breath feels as it enters your nostrils? Now try it again, concentrating on that sensation of cool, dry, and refreshing.

Now play the Kobialka "Pachelbel Kanon" at a reasonable sound level—not too loud or too soft. Close your eyes and once again focus your attention on your nostrils and the sensation of breathing in cool, dry, fresh air.

Good.

Round 3: Repeat the above, but after about the second deep breath, imagine that you are breathing in the music. Imagine that you are not listening to, but breathing in, the music and fill up every space in your body with the music that you are inhaling. When you exhale, slowly pull your abdomen as far back as you can, letting the tension in your body flow out with your breath. Then repeat the inhale procedure. Do this for about four or five breaths.

How do you feel? Many of my clients find this to be an extremely helpful and enjoyable procedure.

You can also combine it with beach imagery by imagining that you are at the beach, listening to the music, and imagining that you are breathing in the music as you are watching the ocean waves. If you have two audio systems, you may wish to superimpose ocean wave sounds on the music.

There are some instances when a more alert state of relaxation is desired. In that case, I use the *Oxygène* piece, with ocean wave sounds superimposed, and my instructions are:

As you inhale, imagine that you are breathing in the music and that it is carrying energy into your body. Feel the energy percolating all through your body. And as you exhale, feel the tension bubbling out with your breath.

I also recommend the "Pachelbel Kanon," or "Jesu, Joy of Man's Desiring," with or without superimposed ocean sounds, when doing

the relaxation sequence, "I'm letting the tension out of my forehead
. . ." (see page 112).

The music and sound selections I have listed here are those that
appeal most to me and to my clients. I have also used *Celtic Harp*,
and other pieces. You will want to experiment and find the ones that
please and relax you best.

Music Facilitates Abdominal Breathing

I have used the pieces mentioned above with numerous clients. With
very few exceptions, they have reported to me that they like the music and that they find it helps them to relax more quickly. It invariably slows down the breathing cycle. This means that the volume of
air increases with each breath, and that less work is being done to
move air in and out of the lungs. This promotes relaxation.

AFTERWORD

Breathing both affects and is, in turn, affected by stress, by our emotions, by anxiety, and by the many physical conditions and medical disorders which we may suffer. With the exception of specific respiratory problems such as asthma and emphysema, most of these conditions are not directly caused by breathing. Yet when breathing loses its natural rhythm, a chain of biochemical events inside your body can be set in motion, which can increase the frequency and severity of discomfort and symptoms. Therapeutic breathing can lessen these.

I have shown you in this book that many stress-related and emotional problems are worsened when breathing loses its natural rhythm: both the brain and the heart are readily observed to lose their natural rhythm when breathing loses it. Many other organs likewise function less effectively, resulting in discomfort and symptoms.

When breathing loses its natural rhythm and you overbreathe, both subtle and not-so-subtle events in your body require immediate compensation. This additional internal source of stress related to maintaining the body's acid-base balance affects metabolism and the function of virtually all organs in your body.

Unless these compensatory changes become drastic, as in kidney disease, diabetes, and heart disease, where aggressive medical attention is required, these compensatory and stressful changes can cause you to just plain not feel well much of the time.

What this means is that you're not sick by medical standards, but you're not well either. And so as you pursue medical diagnoses and treatments, you may find yourself labeled a crank or a hypochondriac.

There are cranks and hypochondriacs, of course. But there are also a lot of people who may have fallen between the cracks of medical knowledge. Perhaps if you're one of those who has fallen into that category, attention to breathing and to breathing-related nutrition may help you.

Remember, you are not *responsible*, in the ordinary sense of that word, for having acquired one or more of these conditions. You could not, at will, acquire a disorder to which you do not have a predisposition by virtue of genetic inheritance. That means if there is absolutely no history of allergies in your family, the chance that you will have one is slim indeed. That also holds for migraine—if there is no evidence of vascular disease in your family, you probably will not suffer from migraine.

No matter how emotionally upset you become, you cannot readily produce a disorder which does not run in your family in one form or another. The disorders described in this book commonly result from an increase in the likelihood or severity of conditions to which you are already predisposed when you make chronic unreasonable demands of your body, such as stress in the form of sustained arousal, poor nutrition, and disordered breathing.

A program that includes sound medical advice, nutrition, and exercises and that focuses on restoring physiological calm and order through deep diaphragmatic breathing with imagery and music may be very helpful in reducing the frequency and severity of the symptoms of your disorders—and, it is hoped, ultimately getting rid of them for good.

While you may not be responsible for acquiring your disorder, you can take responsibility for controlling it, even for reducing it.

Deep abdominal breathing, as taught in this book, has been shown to be an important component in achieving well-being, and music has a profoundly salutary effect on breathing. It helps to increase ventilation, and seems to help reduce the effort or work required by the body to gain air. Listening to music is also a fun way to practice breathing. I hope that in addition to finding these exercises helpful, you will also enjoy doing them.

NOTES

Chapter 1   You Want to Be Well, Don't You?

1. D. Goleman, "The Mind over the Body," *New York Times*, September 27, 1987.

2. M. F. Oliver, "Risks of Correcting the Risks of Coronary Disease and Stroke with Drugs," *New England Journal of Medicine* 306 (1982):297–298.

Chapter 3   The Hyperventilation Syndrome

1. H. Selye, *Stress Without Distress* (Philadelphia: Lippincott, 1974), 108.

2. Ibid., 129.

3. W. F. Evans, Men*tal Medicine* (Boston: H. H. Carter, 1890), 37.

4. I. P. Pavlov, *Conditioned Reflexes* (New York: Oxford University Press, 1927), 506.

5. D. S. Krantz and D. C. Glass, "Personality, Behavior Patterns, and Physical Illness: Conceptual and Methodological Issues," in *Handbook of Behavioral Medicine*, ed. W. D. Gentry (New York: Guilford Press, 1984).

6. H. E. Walker, "Brief Guide to Office Practice," *Medical Aspects of Human Sexuality* 19 (1985):139–148.

7. The pH of a substance is an index of whether it is acid, neutral, or base: 7.0 is neutral, below 7.0 is acid, and above 7.0 is alkaline (base). See B. A. Shapiro, R. A. Harrison, and J. R. Walton, *Clinical Application of Blood Gases* (Chicago: Yearbook Medical Publishers, 1982).

8. As early as 1924, Dr. Joshua Rosett showed that "overventilation" can lead to epileptic seizures. Cited in R. Fried, *The Psychology and Physiology of Breathing in Behavioral Medicine, Clinical Psychology and Psychiatry* (New York: Plenum Press, 1993).

9. U. Gottstein, W. Berghoff, K. Held, H. Gabriel, T. Textor, and U. Zahn, "Cerebral Metabolism during Hyperventilation and Inhalation

of CO_2," in *Proceedings of the Fourth International Symposium on Regulation of Cerebral Blood Flow*, ed. R. W. R. Russel (London: Pitman, 1970).

10. L. C. Lum, "The Syndrome of Habitual Hyperventilation," in *Modern Trends in Psychosomatic Medicine*, ed. O. W. Hill (London: Butterworth, 1976).

11. W. J. Kerr, J. W. Dalton, and P. A. Gliebe, "Some Physical Phenomena Associated with Anxiety States and Their Relationship to Hyperventilation," *Annals of Internal Medicine* 11 (1937):961–992.

12. E. O. Wheeler, P. D. White, E. W. Reed, and M. E. Cohen, "Neurocirculatory Asthenia (Anxiety Neurosis, Effort Syndrome, Neurasthenia)," *Journal of the American Medical Association* 142 (1950):878–889.

13. T. P. Lowry, *Hyperventilation and Hysteria* (Springfield, Ill.: Charles C. Thomas, 1967).

14. L. C. Lum, "Hyperventilation—The Tip and the Iceberg," *Journal of Psychosomatic Research* 19 (1975):375–383; J. C. Missri and S. Alexander, "Hyperventilation Syndrome: A Brief Review," *Journal of the American Medical Association*, 240 (1978):2093–2096; B. I. Lewis, "Hyperventilation Syndrome: Clinical and Physiological Observations," *Postgraduate Medicine* 53 (1957):259–271.

15. *Physicians' Desk Reference* (Montvale, N.J.: Medical Economics Co., 1989).

Chapter 5   Nutrition and Breathing

1. T. W. Clarke, "Epilepsy of Allergic Origin," *New York State Medical Journal* 34 (1934):647–651; J. A. Beauchemin, "Allergic Reaction in Mental Disease," *American Journal of Psychiatry* 92 (1936):1191–1204; H. H. Davison, "Allergy of the Nervous System," *Quarterly Review of Allergy and Immunology* 6 (1952):157–186.

2. C. M. Pemberton, K. E. Moxness, M. J. German, J. K. Nelson, and C. F. Gastineau, *Mayo Clinic Diet Manual* (Toronto: B. C. Decker, 1988), 198.

3. N. P. Sen, "Analysis and Significance of Tyramine Foods," *Journal of Food Science* 34 (1969):22–26.

4. J. Egger, C. M. Carter, J. Wilson, M. W. Turner, and J. F. Soothill, "Is Migraine a Food Allergy? A Double-Blind Controlled Trial of Oligoantigenic Diet Treatment," *Lancet* 2 (1983):865–869.

5. Adapted from Davison, "Allergy of the Nervous System; Egger et al., "Is Migraine a Food Allergy?"; W. Lovenberg, *Some Vaso- and Psy-*

choactive Substances in Food Amines, Stimulants, Depressants, and Hallucinogens Occurring Naturally in Food, 2nd ed. (Washington, D.C.: National Academy of Sciences, 1973); and J. A. Udenfriend et al., "Physiologically Active Amines in Common Fruits and Vegetables," *Archives of Biochemistry and Biophysics* 85 (1959):487.

6. J. Egger, C. M. Carter, J. F. Soothill, and J. Wilson, "Oligoantigenic Diet Treatment of Children with Epilepsy and Migraine," *Journal of Pediatrics* 114 (1989):51–58.

7. R. Fried and R. M. Carlton, "Intracellular Magnesium Deficiency in Epilepsy," *Journal of the American College of Nutrition* (abstr.) 4 (1983): 429–430.

8. C. C. Pfeiffer, *Zinc and Other Micronutrients* (Old Greenwich, Conn.: Devin Adair, 1973).

Chapter 6 Breathing Applications in Common Complaints

1. R. Fried, "Relaxation with Biofeedback-Assisted Guided Imagery: The Importance of Breathing Rate as an Index of Hypoarousal," *Biofeedback and Self-Regulation* 12 (1987):273–278.

2. J. R. Marshall, "Hyperventilation Syndrome or Panic Disorder—What's in the Name?" *Hospital Practice* 22 (1987):105–118.

3. C. Patel, "Randomized Controlled Trial of Yoga and Biofeedback in Management of Hypertension," *Lancet* 2 (1975):93–95.

4. A. Hauptmann and A. Myerson, "Studies of Finger Capillaries in Schizophrenia and Manic-Depressive Psychoses," *Journal of Nervous and Mental Diseases* 108 (1948):81–108.

5. R. R. Freedman and S. Woodward, "Behavioral Treatment of Menopausal Hot Flushes: Evaluation by Ambulatory Monitoring," *American Journal of Obstetrics and Gynecology* 17 (1992):305–306.

Chapter 7 Breathing, Hypertension, and the Heart

1. L. G. Tirala, *The Cure of High Blood Pressure by Respiratory Exercises* (New York: B. Westermann, [1928?]).

2. D. Grady, "A Silent Killer Returns, Doctors Rethinking Tactics to Lower Blood Pressure," *New York Times,* July 14, 1998, F1, F5, F7.

3. D. W. Evans and L. C. Lum, "Hyperventilation as a Cause of Chest Pain Mimicking Angina," *Practical Cardiology* 7 (1981):131–136.

4. C. E. Wheatley, "Hyperventilation Syndrome: A Frequent Cause of Chest Pain," *Chest* 68 (1975):195–199.

5. H. J. Levine, "Mimics of Coronary Disease," *Postgraduate Medicine* 64 (1978):58–67.

6. B. D. Christensen, "Studies on Hyperventilation: II. Electrocardiographic Changes in Normal Man During Voluntary Hyperventilation," *Journal of Clinical Investigation* 25 (1947):880–889.

7. A. Hymes and P. Nuernberger, "Breathing Patterns Found in Heart Attack Patients," *The Research Bulletin of the Himalayan International Society* 2 (1980):10–12.

Chapter 8 Breathing Problems, Anxiety, and Depression

1. A. S. Loeventhal, W. F. Lorenz, H. G. Martin, and J. Y. Malone, "Stimulation of Respiration by Sodium Cyanid and its Clinical Application," *Archives of Internal Medicine* 21 (1918):109–129.

2. O. Clausen, "Respiratory Movements in Normal, Neurotic, and Psychotic Subjects," *Acta Psychiatrica Scandinavica* suppl (1951):168.

3. J. E. Finesinger, "The Effect of Pleasant and Unpleasant Ideas on the Respiratory Pattern (Spirogram) in Psychoneurotic Patients," *American Journal of Psychiatry* 100 (1944):659–667.

4. J. Damas Mora, L. Grant, P. Kenyon, M. K. Patel, and F. A. Fenner, "Respiratory Ventilation and Carbon Dioxide Levels in Syndromes of Depression," *British Journal of Psychiatry* 129 (1976):457–464.

5. H. R. Lazarus and J. J. Kostan, "Psychogenic Hyperventilation and Death Anxiety," *Psychosomatics* 10 (1969):14–22.

6. D. M. Clark, P. M. Salkovskis, and A. J. Shakley, "Respiratory Control as a Treatment for Panic Attacks," *Biological Psychology* 16 (1983): 285–297.

7. G. A. Hibbert, "Hyperventilation as a Cause of Panic Attacks," *British Medical Journal* 288 (1984):263–264.

Chapter 9 Asthma

1. E. R. McFadden and H. A. Lyons, "Arterial Blood Gas Tension in Asthma," *New England Journal of Medicine* 278 (1968):1027–1032.

2. M. G. Belvisi, C. D. Stretton, M. Yacoub, and P. J. Barnes, "Nitric Oxide Is the Endogenous Neurotransmitter of Bronchodilator Nerves in Humans," *European Journal of Pharmacology* 210 (1992):221–222.

3. P. J. Barnes and M. G. Belvisi, "Nitric Oxide and Lung Disease," *Thorax* 48 (1993):1034–1043.

4. S. A. Kharitonov, D. Yates, R. A. Robbins, R. Logan-Sinclair, E. A. Shinebourne, and P. J. Barnes, "Increased Nitric Oxide in Exhaled Air of Asthmatic Patients," *Lancet* 343 (1994):133–135; S. A. Kharitonov, B. J. O'Connor, D. J. Evans, and P. J. Barnes, "Allergen-Induced Late Asthmatic Reactions Are Associated with Exhaled Nitric Oxide," *American Journal of Respiratory and Critical Care Medicine* 151 (1995):1894–1899.

5. S. A. Kharitonov, G. Lubec, M. Hjelm, and P. J. Barnes, "L-Arginine Increases Exhaled Nitric Oxide in Normal Human Beings," *Clinical Sciences* 88 (1995):135–139.

Chapter 10   Migraine, Epilepsy, and Associated Disorders

1. D. J. Dalessio, ed., *Wolff's Headache and Other Head Pain* (New York: Oxford University Press, 1980).

2. R. Low, *Migraine* (New York: Owl Books, 1987).

3. W. K. Amery, "Brain Hypoxia: The Turning-Point in the Genesis of the Migraine Attack?" *Cephalgia* 2 (1982):83–109.

4. E. Harrington in *Migraine—Clinical and Research Aspects*, ed. J. N. Blau (Baltimore: Johns Hopkins University Press, 1987).

5. J. G. Keevil, H. Osman, N. Maalej, and J. D. Folts, "Grape Juice Inhibits Human Ex Vivo Platelet Aggregation while Orange Juice and Grapefruit Juices Do Not," *Journal of the American College of Cardiology* suppl A, 31 (1998):172A.

6. B. F. Feingold, *Introduction to Clinical Allergy* (Springfield, Ill.: Charles C. Thomas, 1973).

7. W. Penfield and H. Jasper, *Epilepsy and the Functional Anatomy of the Brain* (Boston: Little, Brown, 1964).

8. C. W. Darrow and C. C. Graf, "Relation of Encephalogram to Photometrically Observed Vasomotor Changes in the Brain," *Journal of Neurophysiology* 8 (1945):449–461.

9. R. Fried, S. R. Rubin, R. M. Carlton, and M. C. Fox, "Behavioral Control of Intractable Idiopathic Seizures: I. Self-Regulation of End-Tidal Carbon Dioxide," *Psychosomatic Medicine* 46 (1984):315–332.

10. K. Lafferty, J. C. De Trafford, V. C. Roberts, and L. T. Cotton, "On the Nature of Raynaud's Phenomenon: The Role of Histamine," *Lancet* 2 (1983):313–315.

11. F. Deutsch, O. Ehrentheil, and O. Pierson, "Capillary Studies in Raynaud's Disease," *Journal of Laboratory and Clinical Medicine* 26 (1941): 1729–1750.

12. A. Hauptmann and A. Meyerson, "Studies of Finger Capillaries in Schizophrenia and Manic-Depressive Psychoses," *Journal of Nervous and Mental Diseases* 108 (1948):81–108.

13. A. B. Olston, *Mind Power and Privileges* (New York: Crowell, 1902).

14. M. B. Sterman, "Effect of Sensorimotor EEG Feedback Training on Sleep and Clinical Manifestations of Epilepsy," in *Biofeedback and Behavior*, eds. J. Beatty and E. Legewie (New York: Plenum, 1977).

Chapter 11   Music and Breath: A Sound Connection

1. A. Kasamatsu and T. Hirai, "An Electroencephalographic Study of Zen Meditation (Zazen)," *Psychologia* 12 (1969):205–225.

2. See H. Benson, *The Relaxation Response* (New York: Avon Books, 1975).

3. I. A. Taylor and F. Paperte, "Current Theory and Research in the Effects of Music on Behavior," *Journal of Esthetics* 17 (1958):51–58.

4. D. Campbell, *The Mozart Effect* (New York: Avon Books, 1997).

5. S. Halpern with L. Savary, *SoundHealth* (New York: Harper & Row, 1985).

6. H. A. Lingerman, *The Healing Energies of Music* (Wheaton, Ill.: Theosophical Publishing House, 1983).

7. Randall McClellan, *The Healing Forces of Music* (Amity, N.Y.: Amity House, 1988).

8. H. Bonny with L. Savary, *Music and Your Mind: Listening with a New Consciousness* (New York: Harper & Row, 1973).

9. McClellan, *The Healing Forces of Music*, 183–184.

10. D. Schuster, *Your Emotions and Your Health* (Emmaus, Pa.: Rodale Press, 1986).

11. Ibid.

12. S. Halpern with L. Savary, *SoundHealth*.

13. J. Kwalwasser, *Exploring the Musical Mind* (New York: Coleman-Ross, 1955).

14. G. Harrer and H. Harrer, "Music, Emotion and Autonomic Function," in *Music and the Brain*, ed. M. C. Critchley and R. A. Henson (Springfield, Ill.: Charles C. Thomas, 1977).

15. S. Halpern with L. Savary, *SoundHealth*.

INDEX